A Short Treatise on Prayer;

The Great Means of Obtaining From God
Eternal Salvation,
And All the Graces We Stand in Need

By St Alphonsus Liguori

Most Useful for All Classes of Christians
Translated from the Italian
BY A CATHOLIC CLERGYMAN

DUBLIN
Printed by John Coyne, 24 Cooke St

1834

ISBN: 978-0-9819901-0-1

The type in this book is the property of
St Athanasius Press and except for brief
excerpts, may not be reproduced in whole
or in part without permission in writing
from the publisher.

Published by:
St Athanasius Press
133 Slazing Rd
Potosi, WI 53820
melwaller@gmail.com
www.stathanasiuspress.com

Specializing in reprinting Catholic Classics

Check out our available Titles at the
end of this book!

CONTENTS

Introduction Highly Important to the Reader 5
Chapter 1 On the Necessity of Prayer 9
Chapter 2 On the Efficacy of Prayer 30
Chapter 3 On the Conditions of Prayer 41
Chapter 4 On the Humility of Prayer 47
Chapter 5 On the Confidence of Prayer 53
Chapter 6 On the Perseverance Necessary for Prayer 66
Abridgment of Part II 74
God wills that all men be saved, and that no one perish
God invites and commands all sinners to return to Him
Jesus Christ has died for all men, and has offered to His eternal Father for each one, the price of His redemption
Appendix 88
A Prayer to Obtain Final Perseverance 88
A Prayer to Jesus Christ to Obtain His Holy Love 89
A Prayer to Obtain Confidence in the Merits of Jesus Christ, and in the Intercession of Mary 90
Devout Acts to be Made to the Visit of the Blessed Sacrament and to the Image of the Blessed Virgin Mary 91
The Hymn, Pange Lingua, in English 96
Visit to Mary, Mother of God 98
The Hymn, Pange Lingua, in Latin 98
Adoro te Devote 100

DEDICATED TO JESUS AND MARY

O Incarnate Word! You have given Your blood and Your life, to merit for our prayers efficacy to obtain whatever we ask and O God, we are so careless about our eternal destiny, that we will not take the trouble to beg the graces necessary for salvation. You have given us, by means of Prayer, the key of all the divine treasures; and we, through neglect of Prayer, continue in our misery and wretchedness! Enlighten us, O Lord, and make us understand how efficacious our supplications are before Your eternal Father, when they are presented to Him in Your name, and through Your merits. I dedicate to You this little book; bless it, O Lord, and grant that all into whose hands it shall fall, may pray continually, and may exert themselves to stir up in others, the spirit of constant prayer, that they too, may avail themselves of that great means of salvation.

To you, also, O Mary, great mother of God, I commend this little work: extend to it your protection, by obtaining for all who shall read it, the spirit of Prayer, the grace to have recourse always, and in all their necessities, to your Son, and to you, who are the dispenser of grace, and the mother of mercy,--to you, who know not how to leave in sorrow any of those who recommend themselves to your prayers,--to you, who are that powerful Virgin, who obtains from God, for her servants, whatever she asks.

INTRODUCTION,

HIGHLY IMPORTANT TO THE READER

I have already published several spiritual works, viz.: Visits to the Blessed Sacrament, the Clock of the Passion of Jesus Christ, the Glories of Mary, a volume containing a Refutation of Materialism and Deism, and several small Treatises of Devotion, a Novena of the Nativity, which treats of the infancy of our Lord, a Book on the eternal maxims entitled, a Preparation for Death, which contains a great deal of useful matter, for Sermons and Meditations, and also nine Discourses for the time of public calamities. But of all these works, I do not consider one more useful than this little book which treats of prayer as a secure and necessary means of obtaining salvation and all the graces necessary for it. Were it in my power, I would publish as many copies of this little work as there are Christians on earth, and would give to each a copy, that each might be convinced of the absolute necessity of prayer for salvation.

I speak in this manner of this little treatise, because on the one hand, I see the absolute necessity of prayer so strongly inculcated in every page of Holy Writ, and in the writings of all the Fathers, and on the other, I perceive that very few Christians make use of that great means of Salvation. What grieves me most is that though there is no practice of which preachers, confessors, or spiritual writers, should insist with greater warmth, or in stronger terms than on that of prayer. Still, I know that preachers seldom recommend it to their auditors, or confessors to their penitents, and that the spiritual books most currently circulated amongst the people do not sufficiently detail its advantages or inculcate its necessity. They indeed suggest many excellent means of preserving sanctifying grace such as to avoid the occasion of sin, to frequent the sacraments, to resist temptations, to hear the word of God, to meditate on the truths of eternity, and other means; all of which are, I admit, most useful. But of what use, I ask, are sermons, meditations, and all the means proposed by masters of spiritual life, without prayer, when Jesus Christ has declared that He will grant His grace only to those who ask it. 'Ask,' He says, 'and you shall receive.' In God's ordinary providence, all our meditations, and good purposes, and promises, will be fruitless without prayer. If we do not pray, we will be for ever unfaithful to all the inspirations of God's Grace, and to all our own promises. Because, to do actual good, to overcome temptation, and to practise virtue; in a word, to observe all the divine precepts, the light which God pours into our souls, and the reflections and resolutions which we ourselves make, are insufficient. The actual assistance of God is moreover necessary, and as we will immediately see, the Almighty grants this actual assistance to those only who pray, and persevere in prayer. The lights we receive, and our own considerations and good purposes enable us actually to pray, when tempted to transgress the divine law, and by prayer to obtain from God actual help, by which we will avoid sin. But if, in temptation, we do not pray, we shall be lost.

I thought it right, dear reader, to say so much by way of preface, on the advantages and necessity of prayer that you may return thanks to God for giving you, by means of this little book, occasion to reflect more seriously on the importance of that great means of salvation by which alone, all adults who are saved, ordinarily obtain the gift of final perseverance. I therefore, exhort you to be grateful to God for this favor. The gift of prayer is an exceedingly great grace. I hope, dear reader, that after having read this little book, you will not neglect for the future to seek God's assistance by prayer, whenever you are tempted to offend Him. If, in your past life, you have fallen into numberless grievous sins, you may be assured, that this was the result of inattention to prayer, and of not imploring the divine aid to repel the temptations by which you were assailed. I pray you to read again and again, this little work, not because it is my production, but because it is a means of salvation which God puts into your hands, giving you thereby a special proof that He wishes you to be saved. And after having perused it, I beseech you to induce as many as possible of your friends, and of the poor with whom you converse, to read it attentively. Let us now commence in the name of the Lord.

The apostle writing to Timothy says, 'I desire, therefore, first of all, that supplications, prayers, intercessions, and thanksgivings be made for all men.'--1 Tim. 2:1. Prayer, says St Thomas, is an elevation of the soul to God. It takes different names according to the objects sought, or the manner in which they are sought. If the object of Prayer be something determinate, it is called petition; if indeterminate, as when we say, 'incline unto my aid, O God,' it is termed supplication. Obsecration is a solemn form of prayer, in which a favor is fervently implored, and in which the grounds on which we expect to be heard are represented; as when we say, 'By thy cross and passion, deliver us, O Lord.' Thanksgiving is a species of prayer, by which we return thanks for the benefits we have received, and by which St Thomas says, we merit greater blessings. Prayer, strictly speaking, signifies according to St Thomas, recourse to God for aid, but in a more extended signification it includes all the above mentioned species. It is in this extended signification that the word Prayer is used in the sequel of this little work.

To acquire a high esteem and affection for this great means of salvation, we must first reflect seriously on its necessity for salvation, and its efficacy when accompanied with the proper conditions to obtain from God all the graces we stand in need of. Hence, in the first part of this little book, I shall treat of the necessity and efficacy of prayer, and of the conditions necessary to render it effectual. In the second part it will be shown that the grace of prayer is given to all, and the mode in which grace ordinarily operates will be pointed out.

CHAPTER I

ON THE NECESSITY OF PRAYER

The Pelagians erroneously asserted that Prayer is not necessary to obtain salvation. Pelagius, the impious author of that heretical sect, maintained that the damnation of the reprobate should be exclusively attributed to the negligence to acquire a knowledge of the truths necessary to be believed. 'He,' says St Augustine, 'discussed every subject except Prayer,' and prayer, as that holy father taught in conformity with the doctrine of St James, is the only means of obtaining the science of the saints. 'If any of you,' says the apostle, 'want wisdom, let him ask of God who gives to all abundantly, and upbraids not.'--St James 1:5

The Holy Scriptures clearly point out the necessity of Prayer for salvation. 'We ought,' says the Redeemer, 'always to pray, and not to faint.'--Luke 18:1. 'Watch you and pray that you enter not into temptation.'--Matt 26:41. 'Ask, and it shall be given unto you.'--Matt 7:7. The generality of Theologians say that the words, 'We ought,' 'Watch you,' 'Ask,' denote a rigid precept, and the strict necessity of prayer. Wickliffe, erroneously maintaining that every good work is a prayer, asserted that these passages were to be understood not of Prayer, but of the necessity of good works. But the doctrine of Wickliffe has been expressly condemned by the Church. Hence, the learned Lessius says, that, 'The necessity of Prayer for adults cannot be denied without an error against faith; because it is clear from the scriptures, that Prayer is the only means by which the helps necessary for salvation can be obtained.'--Less. de Just. lib. 2. c. 37. Dub. 3. n. 9. The necessity of Prayer is indeed evident for without the aid of divine grace, we cannot perform any good work. 'Without Me,' says our Lord, 'you can do nothing.'--John 15:5. St Augustine observes that Jesus Christ does not say, without me you can consummate nothing; but, without me you can do nothing; giving us thereby to understand that, without His assistance, we cannot even begin a good work. St Paul teaches that so far from being of ourselves capable of exciting a desire, we cannot even have a thought of doing good; 'Not that we are sufficient to think anything of ourselves, but our sufficiency is from God.'--2 Cor 3:5. The same doctrine is inculcated in numberless other parts of scripture: 'God who works all in all.'--1 Cor 12:6. 'I will cause you to walk in my commandments, and to keep my judgments, and do them.'--Ezec 36:27. Hence, St Leo asserts that 'Man does no good which God does not assist him to do.'--St Leo, in Con. Auris, Canon 20. And the Council of Trent says, 'If anyone shall assert that without the preventing inspiration of the Holy Ghost, and His assistance, man can believe, hope, love, or repent as he ought in order to obtain the grace of justification, let him be anathema.'--Sess. 6 Can. 3.

The author of the imperfect work (speaking of the brute creation) says that for their protection, the Almighty has provided some of them with swiftness, some with claws, and others with wings, but man he has made so that God Himself should be his strength.--Auctor op. imperf. Hom. 18. Thus, God having determined that whatsoever man has or can have, should come from divine grace alone, man is utterly incapable of saving his soul by his own powers. God, in His ordinary providence according to Gennadius, gives the assistance of His grace to those only who pray for it: 'We believe,' he says, 'that no one advances towards salvation, but by God's invitation, that no one, though invited, works out his salvation, but by God's assistance, and that he alone who prays merits aid from God.'--Gennad. lib. de Ecel. Dogm. inter opera, St Augus. Since, then, it is certain, on the one hand, that without succor from above we can do nothing, and, on the other, that succor is ordinarily given to him only who prays, is it not evident that prayer is absolutely necessary for salvation? St Augustine admits that some graces, such as the grace of vocation to the faith and to repentance, are given without cooperation, but he asserts that other graces, and especially the gift of perseverance, are granted only to humble and fervent supplication. 'God bestows some favors without prayer, such as the beginning of faith; others, such as perseverance, He has prepared for those only who pray.'--St Aug lib. de persev. cap. 5. Hence the greater number of theologians, after St Basil, St Chrysostom, St Clement of Alexandria, St Augustine, and other fathers, maintain, that Prayer is necessary not only, because in the ordinary dispensations of Providence, without recommending himself to God, and imploring the graces necessary for salvation, no adult can be saved.

'To enter heaven,' says St Thomas, 'continual prayer is necessary after baptism; for although all sins are remitted by that sacrament, there still remains concupiscence to assail us from within, and the world and the devil to attack us from without:' (St Thomas, p. 3, q. 39, a 5.) and to gain eternal life we must not only fight but conquer. 'For the mastery is not crowned except he strive lawfully.'--2 Tim 2:5. But without the divine assistance, which can be obtained only by prayer, we shall not be able to resist the assaults of so many powerful enemies. Hence, without prayer, our salvation is impossible.

That prayer is the only ordinary means of obtaining the gifts of God, the angelic doctor teaches more clearly in another part of his works, (St Thomas, 2. 2. q. 83., a. 2.) where he says, that all the graces which God had prepared for us from eternity will be granted only to prayer. St Gregory says, that 'by prayer men deserve to receive what God from eternity ordained to bestow upon them.'--St Greg. lib. 1, dial. cap. 8. 'Prayer,' says St Thomas, 'is necessary, not to make our wants known to almighty God, but to convince us of our obligation or recur to his mercy for succor and thus to make us acknowledge him to be the author of all our works." (loco cit.) And, as God has ordained the sowing of the seeds of the earth, and the planting of the vine as indispensable means of providing corporal nourishment, so it is His will that we should be able to obtain by prayer only, the graces necessary for the support of spiritual life, and for eternal salvation. 'Ask,' He says, 'and it shall be given unto you; seek and you shall find.'--Matt. 7:7.

In a word, we are but poor mendicants, who have nothing but the alms, which God in his mercy chooses to give us. "But I am," says the Psalmist, "a beggar and poor."--Psalm, 39:18. The Lord, says St Augustine, desires to pour his graces upon us, but not unless we pray: "God wishes to give, but He gives only to him who asks." St Aug. in Ps. 100. "Ask," says Jesus Christ, "and it shall be given." "Whosoever then," says St Teresa, "does not seek, shall not receive." As moisture is necessary to preserve life in plants, and to support their vegetation, "so," says St Chrysostom, "prayer is necessary for the salvation of our soul." "As the body," he says, "cannot live without the soul, so the soul without prayer is dead and fetid."--St Chrysostom, tom. 1. Hom. 67. He says that the soul without prayer, sends forth a bad odor before God, because he who neglects to recommend himself to the divine protection soon begins to put on the corruption of sin. Prayer is also called the nourishment of the soul, because, says St Augustine, as the body cannot be supported without food, so the life of the soul cannot be preserved without prayer. "As the flesh," says the holy doctor, "derives its nutriment from food, so the soul is nourished by prayer." All these similes employed by the fathers show that they considered prayer absolutely necessary for the attainment of salvation.

Besides, prayer is the most necessary weapon of defense against the attacks of our enemies; he that does not wield it, says St Thomas, is lost. The holy doctor did not hesitate to assert that Adam fell, because when tempted, he did not call for aid from above. "He sinned, because he had not recourse to the divine assistance." St Gelasius made a similar assertion with regard to the fall of the rebel angels: "Receiving the grace of God in vain, they could not persevere, because they did not pray."-- Epis. 5. Ad Ep. In Picaeno. Con. Pelag. St Charles Borromeo, in one of his pastoral letters (Act. Eccl. Med. Pag. 1005,) observes, that among all the means of salvation recommended by Jesus Christ in his gospel, prayer has obtained the first place. By prayer He wished the true religion to be distinguished from the religion of all false sects; for He has in a special manner, called His church the house of prayer. "My house shall be called the house of prayer.--Matt. 21:13. St Charles concludes this letter by saying that to prayer may be traced "the beginning, the progress, and the perfection of all virtues." Thus, in the darkness, miseries and dangers by which we are surrounded we can have no ground of hope but in raising our eyes to God, and imploring by humble prayer, his merciful protection. "But as we know not what to do, (said king Josaphat,) we can only turn our eyes to You."--2 Par. 20:12. Holy David not having any other means of escaping the devouring grasp of his enemies, than continually to beseech the Lord to deliver him from their snares, constantly poured forth his supplications for divine aid. "My eyes," said he "are ever towards the Lord; for He shall pluck my feet out of the snare. Look You upon me, and have mercy on me; for I am alone and poor."--Psalm 24:15, 16. And again, "I cried unto You, save me, that I may keep Your commandments."--Psalm 118:146. As if he had said, turn Your eyes, O Lord, toward me; have mercy upon me and save me, for of myself I can do nothing, and except You, there is no one who can deliver me.

And how, after the weakness and infirmity entailed upon us by the sin of Adam, could we resist the violent assaults of our enemies, and observe the law of God, if God had not instituted such a means as prayer, of obtaining sufficient light and grace to fulfill the divine commands? Luther blasphemously asserted that the fall of Adam rendered the observance of the divine law impossible. Jansenius maintained that even the just with the graces which they actually have, cannot observe all the commandments of God. If he had stopped there, his proposition might admit of a favorable explanation; but he proceeded farther, and affirmed that the just have not the grace by which they can render the observance of all the divine precepts possible, and therefore his doctrine has been justly condemned. St Augustine says, that though there are some of the divine precepts, which man, on account of his weakness, cannot fulfill by the aid of the strength which he actually possesses, or of the graces which are given to all, still he can easily obtain by prayer, the assistance necessary for their observance. "God," he says, "does not command impossibilities, but by commanding, He admonishes you to do what you can, and to ask what you cannot do, and He assists you that you may be able to do it."--St Aug. de Nat. & gra. C. 44. N. 50. This celebrated passage has been adopted by the Council of Trent, and the doctrine therein contained confirmed, as a dogma of faith, Sess. 6. C. 11. Immediately after the preceding words, the holy Doctor asks, how can man do what is impossible to him? And he answers that by prayer we obtain from God a remedy for our weakness, and strength to do that which of ourselves we could not accomplish.

We cannot, continues the saint, imagine that God has imposed upon us a law, the fulfillment of which is above our strength; and therefore by making us feel that we are unable to observe His precepts, He admonishes us to do what is easy by the aid of His ordinary grace, and by prayer to obtain additional help to perform what is difficult. "By our faith, which teaches that God cannot command impossibilities, we are admonished what we ought to do in things that are easy, and what to ask in things that are difficult,"--St Aug. de. Nat. & gra. Cap. 69. N. 83. But why, you will ask, has God imposed some precepts, the fulfillment of which is not within our power? That we, replies the saint, may be careful to procure by prayer, assistance to perform what of ourselves we cannot achieve. "He gives some commands with which we cannot comply, to teach us what we ought to ask from Him."--Ibid. cap. 16. N. 3. Again he says, "the law is given, that grace may be sought; grace is given that the law may be fulfilled."--St Aug. in Psalm 502. Without grace, the observance of the law is impossible, and God has given the law to teach us the necessity of constantly imploring the graces necessary for its fulfillment. In another place the holy doctor says, "The law is good, if we make good use of it. How are we to make a good use of it? By acknowledging our own infirmity, and seeking health through the divine assistance."--St Aug. ser. 13. De verb. Apos. C. 3. St Augustine therefore teaches that, by means of the law, the fulfillment of which is impossible to us, we ought to learn our inability to observe its precepts, and that feeling our own impotence, we ought to seek continually by humble prayer, strength from God to heal our weakness. Such also is the doctrine of St Bernard; "Who are we," he says, "or what is our strength, that we should be able to resist so many temptations? God certainly wished that we, seeing that we are deficient, and that out of Him there is no assistance for us, should, with all humility, have recourse to His mercy.--S. Ber. serm. 5. De Quad.

The Almighty is aware how much the necessity of prayer contributes to the exercise of humility, and the confidence in his goodness. Hence he often permits us to be assailed by enemies more powerful than we are, that having recourse to his mercy, we may obtain by prayer strength to repel their attacks. It ought to be particularly remembered, that no one can overcome the temptations of the flesh, without invoking the divine assistance when he is tempted. This frightful enemy by its attacks, covers the soul with darkness, banishes the remembrance of all her meditations and good resolutions, makes her disregard the truths of faith, and extinguishes almost all fear of divine vengeance.

The power of the flesh is strengthened by our natural inclinations, which drag us with the greatest violence to the indulgence of carnal pleasures. St Gregory of Nyssa says that our only defense against this temptation is prayer. "Prayer," he says, "is the safeguard of chastity." Solomon said, "And I knew that I could not otherwise be continent except God gave it: I went to the Lord and besought Him."--Wis. 8:21. Chastity is a virtue which we are unable to practice without the divine assistance, which God gives to those only who ask it from Him. But whosoever prays, will infallibly obtain it. St Thomas observes that we ought not to say that it is impossible to preserve chastity or to observe any of the divine precepts; because, although we cannot by our own strength fulfill the law, yet we can do it by the help of divine grace. 'It must,' he says, 'be said that what we can do by the divine assistance is not at all impossible to us.'--St Thomas 1. 2. q. 109. a. 4. ad. 2. Do not say that it appears unjust to command a lame man to walk erect: no, says St Augustine, such a command is very useful to him, when, by proper exertions, he can obtain a cure for his lameness; and if through sloth he continues lame, he is deserving of censure. It is very expedient to command a lame man "to walk erect, that when he perceives his own inability he may seek a remedy to heal the lameness of sin."--St Aug. de. Perf. Just. Cap. 3.

In fine, he that does not pray as he ought, cannot lead a Christian life. "He," says St Augustine, "knows how to live well who knows how to pray well." St Francis of Assisi says that without prayer no fruit can be expected from the soul. Sinners, then, who say they have not strength to resist temptations, are inexcusable. If, says St James, you have not sufficient strength, why do you not ask for it? "You have it not, because you ask it not."--St James, 4:2. He admits that we are too weak to repel the attacks of our enemies. But it is certain that God is faithful, as the apostle says, and does not permit us to be tempted beyond our strength. "God is faithful, who will not suffer you to be tempted above that which you are able; but will make also with the temptation issue, that you may be able to bear it." --1 Cor 10:13. He will, says Primasius, expounding these words, enable you by the protection of His grace to sustain the temptation. We are weak, but God is strong; by seeking His aid we obtain a participation of His power, and with His strength, according to the apostle, we can do all things: "I can do all things in Him who strengthens me."--Phil 4:13. Hence, says St Chrysostom, he that falls is without excuse; had he continued to pray, he would not have yielded to the enemy.--St Chrysostom, Serm. De Moysi.

Here we may inquire if the intercession of the saints is necessary to obtain the divine assistance. That it is lawful and useful to invoke the saints as intercessors, to ask for us, through the merits of Jesus Christ, the graces which our sins render us unworthy to obtain, has been defined by the Council of Trent. The invocation of the saints was very unjustly censured by the impious Calvin. It is lawful and profitable after the example of the prophet Baruch, and St Paul to ask their aid while living, and to beg of them to assist us by their prayers: "And pray you for us to the Lord our God."--Bar 1:13. "Brethren, pray for us."--1 Thess 5:25. God Himself commanded the friends of Job to beg the prayers of that holy man, that through his merits they might obtain favor; "Go," said He, "to my servant Job; and my servant Job shall pray for you: his face I will accept."--Job 42:8. If then, it is lawful to recommend ourselves to the prayers of the living, why should it not be permitted to invoke the intercession of the saints, who behold God face to face in heaven. As a king may be honored in his servants, as well as in his own person, so the veneration of the saints does not detract from, but adds to, the reverence due to God. It is for this reason, that St Thomas recommends the practice of seeking the intercession of many of the saints: "Because," he says, "sometimes a favor is obtained by the prayers of many which would not be granted to the prayers of one." St Thom in. 4. Sent. Dis. 45. q. 3. a. 2. ad. 2. You will perhaps say that it is useless to invoke the saints, who, without being invoked, intercede for all that are worthy of their prayers. St Thomas answers, that he who is unworthy of their intercession is rendered worthy by praying devoutly to them.--Loc. cit. ad. 5.

The utility of invoking the souls in purgatory is controverted. Some, resting on the authority of Saint Thomas, maintain that they, required to be purified by sufferings, cannot pray for us. Being, he says, in a state of purgation and suffering, they are inferior to us, therefore not in a state to pray for us, but rather in a condition in which they stand in need of our prayers. However Bellarmine, Silvius, Gotti, and others, affirm, with great probability, that we should piously believe that, to preserve a charitable communion of reciprocal prayers between them and us, God makes known to them our prayers. We ought not to infer that because they are not in a state of prayer, they cannot intercede for us; for not to be in a state of prayer, and to be unable to pray, are different things. They indeed as St Thomas says are not in a state of prayer, because being in a state of suffering, they are inferior to us, and stand in great need of our prayers. However, being the friends of God they are capable of praying in our behalf. If a tender parent, in punishment of some fault, incarcerate a beloved son, cannot the son, though unable to obtain his own release intercede for others, and may he not confidently expect that an affectionate father will readily grant his request? So likewise the state of these beloved souls whom God tenderly loves, and whom He has confirmed in grace does not render them incapable of making intercession for us. The Church abstains from invoking their prayers because their state does not afford them any means of knowing that we beg their aid. But it is piously believed that God communicates our wishes to them, and they being full of charity surely will not neglect to present our supplications before the throne of God. When Saint Catherine of Bologna stood in need of any grace, she had recourse to the souls in purgatory, and her prayers were immediately heard; she declared, that through these holy souls, many favors were granted to her which she had sought through the intercession of the saints, and had not obtained.

Here I may be allowed to make a digression in favor of these suffering saints. If we desire the aid of their intercession, it is right that we endeavor to procure a mitigation of their pains by our prayers and good works. I only say that it is right to assist them by our prayers, but to pray for them ought to be regarded as a Christian duty; for charity obliges us to relieve the wants of our neighbor, when we can do it without great inconvenience. Now it is certain among our neighbors are to be numbered the souls in purgatory, who, though no longer in this life, share in the communion of saints, and are therefore reckoned to be among our neighbors. The souls of the faithful departed, says St Augustine, are not separated from the Church.--S Aug lib. 20. de. Civ. Dei. cap. 9. St Thomas asserts, that "the charity that is the bond of union amongst the members of the Church extends not only to the living, but also to those who die in the Lord." Hence, because the souls in purgatory our are neighbors, we ought, according to our ability, to alleviate their pains; and because their necessity exceeds that of the living members of the Church, it would appear that we are bound by a stricter obligation to contribute to their relief.

Now, what are the necessities of these holy prisoners? It is certain that their pains are exceedingly intense. "The fiery torments," says St Augustine, (S Aug in. Ps. 37.) "which they endure far surpass the most excruciating tortures that man can suffer in this life." St Thomas says, "the damned are tormented, and the elect purified, by the same fire."--S. Thom. in. 4. Sent. Dist. 21. The pain, then, of sense suffered by the souls in purgatory equals, but the pain of loss, or the privation of God's glory far exceeds, that of the damned. For, being inflamed by a natural and supernatural love of God's perfections, they are drawn to Him with such violence, that the consideration of being separated from Him by their own faults, excites sufficient pains to produce, if possible, instant death. St Chrysostom declares that the pain of loss, or the privation of God is infinitely more excruciating than the pain of sense. "A thousand internal fires united together would not cause so much pain as the sole pain of loss." Hence the spouses of Jesus Christ detained in purgatory, would rather undergo all other torments, then suffer their longed for union with God to be delayed for a single moment. St Thomas says, that the pains of purgatory exceeds any pains of this life.--S. Thom. in. 4. Sent. Dis. 21. q. 1. a. 1. q. 3. Dionysius the Carthusian relates, that a certain man raised from the dead by St Jerome, declared to St Cyril of Jerusalem, that in comparison of the least pain suffered in purgatory, all the torments in this world are delights; and that, if a man experienced these pains, rather than undergo the smallest of them, he would submit to all the miseries that the human race will suffer till the day of judgment.--Diony. Char. Noviss. l. 4. p. 3. a. 19. Hence St Cyril says that the pains of purgatory and of hell are equally acute; that they differ only in point of duration. The sufferings, then of these holy souls is excessive; they are incapable of relieving themselves; holy Job says, they are "in chains, and bound with cords of poverty."--Job 36:8. These holy queens are destined to a kingdom, but they are not allowed to take possession of it, till after the term of their purgation. Their chains cannot be loosened until the divine justice is satisfied to the full. Even the theologians who assert that the souls in purgatory can obtain some relief by their own prayers, admit they cannot merit a full remission of their punishment. A Cisterian monk who was in purgatory, said to the Sacristan of his monastery, "Assist me, I beseech you, by your prayers, for of myself I can obtain nothing.--Istor. dell. Ord. Cist. This is conformable to the doctrine of St Bonaventure: "The poverty," he says, "of a beggar renders him unable to pay his debts." S. Bona. Serm. de. Morte. And such is the indigence of these suffering souls, that they have no means of making satisfaction to God's justice.

It is of faith that we can assist them by our suffrages, and particularly by the prayers recommended and used by the Church for their deliverance. For my part, I cannot conceive how a Christian can be excused from sin, who makes no effort to relieve them, even by his prayers. Let us then endeavour to assist them, if not from a sense of duty, at least from the consideration of the satisfaction it will afford Jesus Christ to see us seeking to release from prison, his own beloved spouses, and to obtain their admission into His kingdom; or from a consideration of the treasure of merits we will acquire by practicing so great an act of charity towards these blessed souls. Remember that they are exceedingly grateful; they know the great benefit we confer upon them, when by our prayers we procure a mitigation of their pains, and an anticipation of their admission to glory; and as soon as they take possession of God's kingdom, they will assuredly not neglect to pray for us. If the Lord promises mercy to those who show mercy, ("Blessed are the merciful for they shall obtain mercy."--Matt 5:7.) Surely he that endeavors to alleviate the sufferings of souls so grievously afflicted, and so dear to God, must have strong grounds to hope for salvation. Jonathan, after having saved the Hebrews from ruin by the victory he obtained over their enemies, was condemned to death for having violated the command of his father, by tasting a little honey; but the people went to Saul and said to him: "Shall Jonathan then die, who has wrought this great salvation in Israel? This must not be: As the Lord lives, there shall not one hair of his head fall to the ground. So the people delivered Jonathan that he should not die."--1 Kings 14:45. In like manner we may expect that, if any one among us obtain by his prayers, the liberation of a soul from purgatory, and her admission into Paradise, that soul will appear in his behalf before the face of God, saying, Lord do not suffer to be lost the man who has freed me from pain and agony. And if Saul spared the life of Jonathan at the request of the people, surely God will not refuse eternal salvation to a Christian, for whose immortal happiness are offered the supplications of a soul which is the spouse of Jesus Christ. Besides, St Augustine says, that they who in this life contribute most to the relief of the faithful departed, will during their own purgatory, by the dispensation of Providence, receive the greatest succor from the prayers of the Church Militant. I may here observe that it affords very great comfort to the souls in purgatory to hear mass for their repose, and during that holy sacrifice to recommend them to God through the merits of the passion of Jesus Christ, saying, "Eternal Father, I offer you this sacrifice of the body and blood of Jesus Christ, along with all the pains which he suffered in His life and death; and through the merits of His passion, I recommend to you all the souls in purgatory, and especially N. N." It is an act of very great charity to pray, at the same time, for the souls who are in their last agony.

Whatever doubts may be entertained about the utility of recommending ourselves to the prayers of the souls in purgatory, or about their ability to intercede for us, it cannot be questioned that the invocation of the saints canonized by the Church, and in the enjoyment of eternal glory, is most useful. St Bonaventure, Bellarmine, and others maintain, that it would be heresy to disbelieve the infallibility of the Church in the canonizations of saints; and every Catholic will agree with Suares, Azorius, and Gotti that to propound such a disbelief would be at least, a very close approximation to heretical doctrine. For as St Thomas teaches, the sovereign pontiff, in proposing saints to the veneration of the faithful, is guided by the infallible influence of the Holy Ghost.--St Thomas, quodlib. 9. art. 15, ad. 1.

Let us now return to a question proposed above; namely, whether it be obligatory on Christians to invoke the intercession of the saints? Without intending to give a decisive answer on this point, I will briefly expound the doctrine of St Thomas. First, in many of the passages already cited, and particularly in the book of sentences, he supposes as certain that all Christians are obliged to pray, because, as he asserts, it is by prayer only, they can obtain the graces necessary for salvation. "Each person," he says, "is bound to pray, because it is his duty to procure for himself spiritual goods, which are given only from on high, and can therefore be obtained in no other way than by asking them from God."--St Thom. in 3. sent. dis. 15. q. 4. In another passage of the same book, the angelic doctor asks, "Whether we ought to pray to the saints to intercede for us?" And he answers, "Order is instituted by God according to Dionysius, that things which are remote may be brought to God by those that are intermediate. Hence, since the saints in heaven are very near to God, the order of the divine law requires, that we, who remaining in the body are absent from the Lord, should be brought to Him by their mediation which indeed, happens when the divine Goodness diffuses its effects through the saints. And, because our return to God ought to correspond to the procession of His benefits, because the benefits of God flow unto us through the suffrages of the saints, it is necessary that we be brought back by the saints to God, to partake frequently through their mediation, of His favors. Hence it is, that we constitute them our intercessors with God, and as it were mediators, when we ask them to pray for us."--In. 4 sen. dist. 45. q. 3. Mark the words, "the order of the divine law requires as the benefits of God flow unto us through the suffrages of the saints, so we are brought to God by their prayers that through their mediation, we may frequently receive His benefits." Hence, according to St Thomas, the order of divine law requires that we, who receive through the mediation of the saints, the helps necessary for salvation, should be saved through their intercession. To those who object that God being infinitely more merciful and more willing to hear our prayers than the saints can be, it is superfluous to invoke their assistance, St Thomas answers, that God has ordained the intercession of the saints as a means of salvation, not on account of any defect of divine mercy, but to preserve the universally established order of operating by means of secondary causes.

In conformity with this doctrine of St Thomas, the Continuator of Tournely and Sylvius say that though God alone is to be invoked as the author of grace, still, to observe the order established by Providence for the attainment of salvation, we are bound to have recourse to the intercession of the saints. The order of divine Providence is, that persons of an inferior rank be saved by imploring the aid of those who enjoy a superior dignity. "We are," says the Continuator of Tournely, "bound to observe the order which God has instituted: now God has ordained, that inferiors obtain salvation by supplicating the assistance of superiors."--Con. Tournel. tom. 1. de. Reli. cap. 2. de ora. ar. 4. q. 1. cum Sylvio.

And if to preserve the order established by God, it is a duty to seek the intercession of the saints, how much more strictly are we obliged to invoke the aid of the divine mother, whose intercession is certainly more efficacious than would be, without hers, the intercession of the whole celestial host. For, St Thomas says, that each of the saints, in proportion to his merits, can save many; but that Jesus Christ and His Blessed Mother have merited grace sufficient to save all men.--St Thom. Epis. 8. "By you," says St Bernard, speaking of Mary, "O inventress of grace and mother of salvation, we have access to your Son that He, who through you was given to us, may through you receive us! As if he said, as we have access to the Father only through the Son, who is mediator of justice, so we can approach the Son only through the mother, who is a mediatrix of grace, and who by her intercession obtains for us the graces which Jesus Christ has merited. The same saint, in another place observes, that Mary has received from God a two-fold plenitude of grace. The first was the Incarnation of the divine Word made Flesh in her sacred womb. The second, the plenitude of the graces which, through her advocacy, we receive from God. He then adds, "God has placed the plenitude of all good in Mary, so that whatever hope, or grace, or salvation we have, all comes from her who ascended abounding in delights. She is a delicious garden, whose sweet odors, that is the gifts of grace, are abundantly diffused in all directions!"--S. Ber. Serm. de Aquaeduct. Whatever then we receive from the Lord, is procured by the intercession of Mary. And why? "Because," says St Bernard, "it is the will of Him who has decreed that we should have every thing through Mary." But a stronger reason is drawn from the writings of St Augustine, who says, that Mary is justly called mother of the faithful, the members of the Saviour, because by her charity she has cooperated to the spiritual birth of the members of the head, Christ Jesus."--S. Aug. lib. 3. de Symb. Cat. cap. 4. Hence, as Mary has cooperated by her charity for our regeneration, so God has willed that she could cooperate with us, by her intercession, in obtaining the life of grace in this world, and the life of glory in the next. It is for this reason, that the Church salutes her as our life, our sweetness, and our hope.-- "Vita, dulcedo, spes nostra, salve."

Hence, since the prayers of the divine mother are infallibly heard by her Son, St Bernard strenuously exhorts us to the constant invocation of Mary.--S. Ber. Ser. De Aquaed. "Recur," he says, "to Mary; the Son will assuredly hear the mother." And afterwards he adds, "My little children, she is the ladder of sinners; she is my greatest confidence, and the entire ground of my hope." The saint calls her "the ladder of sinners," because, as the third step is attained only by means of the second, and the second, by means of the first, so we can ascend to the Father only through the Son, and to the Son only through Mary. He then calls her "his greatest security, and the entire ground of his hope;" because, (as he supposes) God wishes that all the graces which he dispenses, should pass through the hands of Mary. He concludes by saying, that since Mary obtains whatsoever she asks, and since her prayers can never be rejected, we should seek, through her intercession, all graces we stand in need of. "Let us," he says, "seek grace, and seek it through Mary; what she asks, she receives, and cannot be refused." The doctrine of St Bernard is conformable to that of St Ephrem, St Ildefonsus, St Germanus, and many others distinguished for sanctity and learning. "We have no other security," says St Ephrem, "than from you, O most sincere Virgin." "The supreme Majesty," says St Ildefonsus, "decreed to entrust to your hands, O Mary, all favors which He determined to bestow on mankind. For to you are committed the treasures and ornaments of graces." "If you desert us," says St Germanus, "what shall become of us, O life of Christians." St Peter

Damian, thus addresses Mary, "In your hands are all the treasures of the mercies of God." St Antonine declares that, "he who asks, without her, attempts to fly without wings." St Bernardine of Sienna, thus salutes her, "O dispenser of all graces, our salvation is in your hand." In another place, he asserts, that not only all graces are transmitted to us through Mary, but that by being made Mother of God, she acquired a certain jurisdiction over all the graces which are distributed among Christians. "The vital graces of Christ," he says, "are transfused through the Virgin into His mystic body by the head, Christ Jesus." As soon as the Virgin Mother conceived in her womb, the Divine Word, she obtained (if I may so speak) a certain jurisdiction over all the gifts of the Holy Ghost, so that no creature has obtained any grace from God, unless according to the dispensation of His pious Mother. Therefore, all gifts, virtues, and graces are dispensed to whom He wills by the hands of Mary. St Bonaventure says, "Since the whole divine nature existed within the womb of the Virgin, I do not hesitate to assert that this Virgin, from whose womb, as from the ocean of the divinity, all the treasures of grace emanate, has a certain jurisdiction over all the effusions of grace." Hence, then, many theologians resting on the authority of these saints, have piously and justly maintained the opinion that no grace is given to man which is not given through the prayers of Mary. This doctrine is taught by Vega, Mendoza, Paciuchelli, Segneri, Poire, Crasset, Natalis, Alexander, and many others. "God," says Natalis Alexander, "wills that we expect to obtain from Him all graces through the most powerful intercession of His Virgin Mother, provided we invoke her as we ought." And in confirmation of his opinion he adduces the above-cited passage of St Bernard: "So He wills, who ordained that we should have every thing through Mary." Father Contensonius, on the words, "Behold your Mother," addressed by Jesus Christ from the cross to St John, comments thus: "As if He said, no person shall be partaker of my blood, but by the intercession of my mother. My wounds are the fountains of grace, but the streams shall flow to none, except through Mary; O my disciple John, you shall be loved by me, in proportion as you will have loved her"--Contens. Theol. Mentis et Cord. to. 2. l. 10. d. 4. cap. 1. If God is pleased by our prayers to the saints, will He not be much more highly gratified by our supplications to Mary to supply, as St Anselm says, our deficiency by her merits. "That the dignity of the intercessor may supply our poverty. Hence the invocation of the Virgin does not proceed from diffidence in the divine mercy, but from a sense of our unworthiness."--S. Ans de Excel. Virg. cap. 6. St Thomas attributes to Mary a dignity almost infinite; "Because," he says, "she is the Mother of God; she has a certain infinite dignity."--S. Thom. 1 par. q. 25. a. 6. ad. 4. Hence, it may be justly asserted that the advocacy of Mary is more powerful before God, than the prayers of the rest of the celestial court.

I close this first point by concluding from what has been said, that he who prays shall be infallibly saved, and that he who does not pray will be inevitably lost. All the elect (infants except) are saved by prayer. All the reprobate are lost through neglect of prayer; if they prayed they should not be lost. Their greatest source of desperation in hell is, and will be for eternity that they had it in their power to save their souls with so much facility by humble prayer, and that now the time of supplication is gone forever.

CHAPTER II

ON THE EFFICACY OF PRAYER

So dear are our prayers to God, that He has destined His angels to present them to Him as soon as they are offered. 'The angels,' says St Hilary, 'preside over the prayers of the faithful, and offer them daily to God.' The prayers of the saints are that sacred smoke of incense which St John saw ascending before the Lord from the hands of the angels.--Apoc. 8. The same apostle, in the fifth chapter of the Apocalypse compares the prayers of the saints to golden vials full of odors, which are exceedingly sweet and acceptable to God. But, to be convinced of the efficacy of prayer before God, it is sufficient to read the numberless promises which He has made in the old as well as in the New Testament, to all who invoke His aid. 'Call upon Me and I will hear."--Job. "Call upon Me in the day of trouble, I will deliver thee."--Psalm 49:15. "Ask and it shall be given unto you: seek and you shall find: knock and it shall be opened to you."--Matt. 7:7. "How much more will your Father who is in heaven, give good things to them that ask."--Matt. 7:11. "For every one that asks, receives; and he that seeks, finds."--Luke, 11:10. "Whatsoever they shall ask, it shall be done for them by my Father."--Matt. 18:19. "All things whatsoever you ask when you pray, believe that you shall receive, and they shall come unto you."--Mark, 11:24. "If you shall ask any thing in my name, that I will do."--John, 14:14. "You shall ask whatsoever you will, and it shall be done to you."--John, 15:7. "Amen, Amen, I say to you; if you ask the Father any thing in my name, He will give it to you."--John, 16:28. A thousand similar passages might be cited, which for the sake of brevity, I omit.

God ardently desires our salvation, but for our greater

good, He wishes that we should be saved by our victories. While on this earth we must live in continual warfare, and to be saved, we must fight and conquer. "No one," says St Chrysostom, "can be crowned without victory."--S Chry. Ser. 1 de Mart. We are very weak; our enemies are numerous and exceedingly powerful; how shall we be able to combat and defeat them: Let each one animate his courage, by addressing to himself the words of the apostle, "I can do all things in Him who strengthens me." We can do all things by prayer, which will procure for us from God strength which we do not possess. Theodoret says that prayer is omnipotent; it is one, but it can do all things: "Oratio cum sit una, omnia potest." St Bonaventure teaches that "by prayer, is obtained possession of every good, and deliverance from every evil." St Lawrence Justinian says, by the practice of prayer we can construct an impregnable citadel in which we shall be securely protected against all the snares and violence of the enemy.--S Lau. Just de Casto. connub. Cap. 22. The powers of hell are strong, but St Bernard says prayer is much stronger. "Prayer, he says, "is more powerful than all the devils;" because by prayer the soul obtains the divine assistance which is infinitely superior to every created power. It was this that encouraged David in all his fears and dangers. "Praising," he said, "I will call upon the Lord: and I shall be saved from my enemies."--Psalm 17:4. "Prayer," says St Chrysostom, "is a great armor, a strong defense, a safe harbor, an inexhaustible treasure."--S Chry. in Psalm 145. Prayer is an armor capable of resisting all the assaults of the devil; it is a defense which preserves us in every danger, a port which saves us in every storm, and a treasure which supplies us with every good.

Knowing the great advantages which we derive from the necessity of prayer, God permits the enemy to assail us, that we may seek the assistance which He offers and promises to us. But the neglect of prayer is as displeasing to God as the invocation of His name in the time of danger is acceptable in His sight. As, says St Bonaventure, a king considers a general to be unfaithful, who when besieged by the enemy does not seek assistance, so God regards as traitors those Christians who, when beset by temptations, do not apply to Him for aid. For He desires to succor them abundantly, and only waits to be asked for support. The willingness of almighty God to grant us the protection we stand in need of, was strikingly evinced in His conduct to the faithless Achaz. He told that king by the mouth of the prophet Isaias, to ask a sign of the readiness and eagerness of the Lord to come to his assistance. "Ask thee a sign of the Lord your God."--Isaias, 7:11. Trusting in his own strength, and expecting to defeat the enemy without the divine aid, the impious king answered, "I will not ask, and I will not tempt the Lord." Isaias, 7:12. But to show how much God is offended by the neglect of those who ask not the graces which He offers, the prophet exclaimed, "Hear you therefore, O house of David: is it a small thing for you to be grievous to men, that you are grievous to my God also."--Isaias, 7:13.

"Come to me all you that labor and are heavy laden, and I will refresh you."--Matt 11:28. My dear children, says the Redeemer, do not lose courage when assailed by your enemies, and oppressed by the weight of your sins, have recourse to Me by prayer, and I will give you strength to resist their attacks, and will repair all your losses. In another place He says by the mouth of Isaias, "come and accuse me, says the Lord: if your sins be as scarlet they shall be made white as snow."--Isaias, 1:18. O you children of men, He says, have recourse to Me; however burdened your consciences may be, do not cease to supplicate My mercy: if, after having called upon Me, I do not give you My grace, and make you white as snow, I shall patiently submit to your reproaches. What is prayer? "Prayer," says St Chrysostom, "is an anchor to those who are tossed by the tempest, it is the treasure of the poor, the remedy of sickness, and the safeguard of health."--S. Chry. Hom. 31. Ad. Pop. An. In the time of storm, prayer is a secure anchor; in poverty, an inexhaustible treasure of riches; in infirmity, a most efficacious remedy; and in health, an infallible preservative. What is the effect of prayer? "It appeases God," says St Laurence Justinian, "it obtains what is asked, it subdues adversaries, it changes men."--S. Laur. Just. de Perf. cap. 12 Prayer pacifies the anger of God, who immediately pardons all who humbly ask forgiveness; it obtains every grace which is sought; it overcomes all the forces of the enemy; and changes men, by giving light to the blind, strength to the weak, and sanctity to sinners. If any one stand in need of light, let him ask from God, and it will be given to him. As soon as I had recourse to God, says Solomon, He granted me wisdom. "I called on the Lord, and the spirit of wisdom came upon me."--Wisd. 7:7. If any one is weak, let him ask for strength, and it will be given to him. As soon as I opened my mouth to pray, says holy David, I obtained succor from God. "I opened my mouth and panted."--Ps. 118:131. And how, except by prayer, which procured strength to overcome torments and death, were the holy martyrs enabled to withstand the persecutions of tyrants.

"Whoever," says St Chrysostom, "practices prayer, fears not death, leaves the earth, enters heaven, and lives with God."--S. Chrys. Ser. 43. He sins not; and divested of every earthly affection, he begins to dwell in heaven, and to enjoy the conversation of God. Why then should such a one be disturbed by vain apprehensions that his name may not be written in the book of life; that God may not give him efficacious graces, or the gift of final perseverance. "Be not," says St Paul, "solicitous about any thing; but in every thing by prayer and supplication, with thanksgiving, let your petitions be known unto God."--Phil. 4:6. Do not allow yourselves to be agitated by groundless fears: banish all uneasiness and solicitude, which only lessen confidence, and increase tepidity and sloth, in the work of salvation. Pray always, make your prayers acceptable to God, thank Him continually for His promises to grant to your prayers efficacious graces, perseverance, salvation, and whatsoever may be necessary for you. The Lord has placed us in battle array to contend with powerful enemies; but He is faithful to His promises, and will not permit their attacks to surpass our strength. "And God is faithful, who will not suffer you to be tempted above that which you are able."--1 Cor 10:13. He is faithful, and instantly affords succor to all who call upon Him. The learned Cardinal Gotti asserts, that "when in our temptations we fly to the divine protection, God is bound to grant strength by which we can and will actually resist; for we can do all things in Him who strengthens us by grace, provided we ask it with humility."--Gotti. Theol. Tom. 2. de grat. tract. 6. q. 2. § 3. n. 30. Being able to procure by humble prayer the divine aid, which will enable us to do all things, we are inexcusable if we yield to temptation. It is our own fault if we be vanquished: our defeats are the result of the neglect of prayer. By prayer we might repel all the attacks of the enemy. "By Prayer," says St Augustine, "all evils are put to flight."--S. Aug. Ser. de Orat.

St Bernadine of Sienna says, that prayer is a most faithful ambassador, well known to the King of heaven, accustomed to enter His chamber, and by its importunity to incline His pious will to grant every assistance to us miserable sinners, who groan amidst combats, and under the weight of our miseries in this valley of tears.--S. Ber. Serm. In Dom. 3. Isaias assures us, that as soon as the Lord hears our prayers, He is moved to compassion; that He does not allow our sorrows to continue long, but instantly grants what we ask from Him. "Weeping you shall not weep; He will surely have pity on you: at the voice of your cry, as soon as He shall hear, He will answer you."--Isa. 30:19. The Lord complains of His people by the Prophet Jeremiah, saying, "Am I become a wilderness to Israel, or a lateward springing land? Why then have My people said, we are revolted, and we will come to You no more?"--Jer. 2:31. Why, says the Lord, do you say you will have recourse to Me no more? Is My mercy a barren land, which can produce no fruits of grace in your behalf? Or a soil which gives its fruit too late? Such is the tender and affecting language in which our loving Lord represents His immediate and unceasing attention to our supplications, and in which He sharply rebukes the tepidity of those who, through diffidence of being heard, abandon prayer.

To be permitted once in the month to present our petitions before the throne of God, would be a great favor. Earthly monarchs seldom give audience to their subjects; but God is ready at all times to listen to the petitions of His servants. St Chrysostom says that "God is always prepared to hear our prayers, and that a petition presented to Him, and accompanied with the necessary conditions, never fails to attain its object." In another place he says that what we ask is obtained before the conclusion of our prayers.--S. Chry. Hom. 52. In (((garbled))). This is confirmed by God's own promise: "As they are yet speaking I will answer."--Isaias, 65:24. The Lord, says David, is near to all who pray to Him, and ready to console, to favor, and save them. The Lord is near to all them that call on Him, to all that call upon Him in truth. He will do the will of them that fear Him, and He will hear their prayer and save them."--Ps. 144:19. It was in the privilege of constant access to the Lord, that Moses gloried. "Neither," said he, "is there any other nation so great, that has God so near them, as our God is present to all our petitions."--Deut. 4:7. The gods of the gentiles being miserable and impotent creatures, disregarded the prayers of their people; but the God of Israel being omnipotent is not inattentive to our cries, but is near to us, and ready to grant all the graces we ask from Him. "In what day soever says the Psalmist, "I shall call upon You, behold I know You are my God."--Ps. 55:11. As if he said, Lord, in this I know You are to me a God of goodness and of mercy, that whensoever I have recourse to You, I shall obtain immediate relief.

We indeed are poor, but by prayer our wants may be speedily supplied. If we are poor, God is rich, and liberal beyond measure, to all who invoke His assistance. "He is rich," says St Paul, "to all who call upon Him."--Rom. 10:12. Since, then our petitions are presented to a God of infinite power, and of infinite riches, let us ask not for trifles, but for valuable and important favors. "You ask from the omnipotent," says St Augustine, "ask for something grand and magnificent." He that asks the king for a trifle, casts an imputation on his power and generosity, and dishonors his majesty. But we honor God, we adore His mercy and liberality when, notwithstanding our misery and our unworthiness to receive any favor from Him, we ask His graces with confidence in His goodness, and in the fidelity of His promises to grant whatever is sought in the name of Jesus Christ. "You shall ask whatever you will, and it shall be done unto you."--John 15:7. St Mary Magdalen de Pazzis says, that God feels honored and consoled, and even grateful, when we ask His graces;

because, by praying to Him we afford Him an opportunity of pouring out His benefits, and manifesting His bounty, which prompts Him to bestow His favors on all. We may be persuaded that He always grants more than we ask. "But if any one," says St James, "wants wisdom, let him ask of God, who gives to all men abundantly, and upbraids not."--St James 1:5. St James speaks in this manner to denote, that God does not, like man, dispense His favors with a parsimonious hand. Human riches being finite are diminished by every contribution to the poor; and therefore men, however opulent, compassionate, and liberal are always sparing of their alms, and seldom grant the full prayer of their petitioners. But the treasures of God being infinite, the more He bestows, the more He still has to give; and therefore He distributes His graces with a liberal hand, always granting more than is sought. "For You, O Lord are sweet and mild, and plenteous to all that call upon You."--Ps. 85:5. You, O my God, said holy David are sweet and liberal beyond measure to all who invoke you; the superabundant mercies which you pour down upon your servants far exceed their demands.

Being assured, then, that prayer opens all the treasures of heaven, we should be careful to pray with unbounded confidence. "Let us attend to this," says St Chrysostom, "and we shall open heaven to ourselves." Prayer is a treasure from which each derives advantages in proportion to the frequency and fervor of his supplications. St Bonaventure says that a Christian, as often as he has recourse to God by fervent prayer, obtains graces which are more valuable than the entire world.--S. Bon. In Luc. 18. There are some fervent souls who devote a great deal of time to reading and meditation, but attend very little to prayer. Spiritual reading and mediation are certainly very profitable; but St Augustine says that prayer is much more beneficial to the soul. Spiritual reading and meditation teach us our obligations, but prayer obtains grace to fulfill them. "Prayer" says St Augustine, "is better than reading; by reading we learn what we ought to do, by prayer we receive what we ask."--S. Aug. in Ps. 75. To know our duties and not perform them only renders us more guilty before God. Though our spiritual lectures and meditations should be very long and frequent, we shall never discharge our duties, unless we ask God's assistance to fulfill them.

Hence, observes St Isidore, the devil is never so vigorous in his efforts to suggest to our minds worldly thought as when we are employed in seeking God's grace by holy prayer, and why? Because the enemy sees that it is by prayer we procure the choicest gifts of heaven. The principal advantage of meditation is, that it stimulates us to ask of God the graces necessary for perseverance and for eternal salvation. Hence, the chief reason of the moral necessity of mental prayer to preserve the life of grace is that he who is not reminded by meditation of his obligation to pray for the helps necessary for perseverance and eternal life, will never remember it: unless he meditates he will never think of the necessity of seeking assistance from above, and therefore will never ask it. But he that meditates every day, perceives his own wants; he sees the dangers by which he is encompassed, and the absolute necessity of prayer to save his soul. The lights received in meditation teach him to pray, and by prayer he will obtain grace which will ensure his perseverance and salvation. Father Segneri said that in the beginning of his mental prayer, which was long and frequent, he was accustomed to direct his efforts more to the excitation of pious affections than to humble petition; but being convinced in the course of his reflections, of the necessity and immense advantages of prayer, he then generally devoted the remainder of his meditation to fervent supplication of God's mercy.

"I will cry like a young swallow," (Is. 328:14) said the devout king Ezechias. As the young swallow is continually crying to its mother for help and food, so should our prayers and tears if we desire to preserve the life of grace, be constantly poured forth to God for protection against the death of sin, and for assistance to advance in His holy love. Father Rodriguez relates that the ancient Fathers, the first spiritual masters, having consulted together came to the conclusion that the best and most indispensable means of salvation consisted in the frequent repetition of the short prayer of holy David. "Incline unto my aid, O God." With them Cassian agrees; he says that whoever desires to be saved, should be continually occupied in reciting the following prayer: Assist me, O my God; assist me, O my God. We ought to begin the day by reciting that prayer the instant we awake; we should repeat it, in all our necessities, in all our occupations spiritual as well as temporal, and especially when we are molested by any passion or temptation. St Bonaventure says that sometimes grace is more readily obtained by one short prayer than by many good works.--S. Bon. de Prof. rel. lib. 2. c. 68. "Sometimes", he says, "a person very easily procures by a short prayer what he would scarcely obtain by pious works." St Ambrose declares that he who asks receives while he is praying, because to pray and to receive are one and the same! S. Am. 84. ad. Demet. Hence, St Chrysostom asserts that "nothing is more powerful than a man who prays," because he partakes of the power of God. St Bernard teaches that to arrive at perfection, prayer and meditation are necessary; by meditation we see our wants, and through prayer we receive what is necessary for us. "Let us," he says, "ascend by meditation and prayer; the former points out what is wanted, and the latter obtains it."-

-S. Ber. ser. 1. de S. Andrea.

In a word, to be saved without prayer is as we have seen, most difficult, and in God's ordinary providence, impossible. But prayer renders salvation most easy and secure. To be saved, it is not necessary, like the martyrs, to expose our lives for the faith; nor, like the holy anchorets, to retire into the desert, and live on wild herbs. No; it is sufficient to send forth our cries frequently to heaven, saying, Assist me, O Lord; O my God, assist me and have mercy on me: and what more easy than continually to invoke the Lord? St Laurence Justinian exhorts us to make an effort to pray at least at the beginning of all our actions. "We should," he says, "endeavour to pour forth our prayer in the beginning at least of every work." Cassian says that the ancient Fathers recommended in a particular manner, the practice of having recourse to God by short but frequent prayers. "Let no person," says St Bernard, "make little of his prayer, since God sets a high value on it; He will give what we ask, or what He knows will be more useful to us."--S. Ber. Serm. 5. de Quad. If we do not pray, we shall certainly be without excuse; for the grace of prayer is given to all, it is in our power to pray whenever we wish. "With me," says David, "is prayer to the God of my life; I will say to God, You are my support."--Ps. 41:9-10. This point is fully discussed in the second part of this work in which it is clearly demonstrated that God bestows on all the grace of prayer, to enable them by pious supplications to obtain abundant aid to observe the divine law, and to persevere unto death in God's service. For the present, I will only say, that if we be not saved, it will be our own fault: we shall be lost only because we shall not have prayed.

CHAPTER III

ON THE CONDITIONS OF PRAYER

"Amen, I say to you, if you ask the Father anything in My name, He will give it to you."--St John 16:23. Jesus Christ then has promised that when our prayers are accompanied with the requisite conditions, whatever we ask the Father in His name, shall be given to us. "You," says St James, "ask and receive not; because you ask amiss."--St James 4:3. In conformity with this doctrine of the apostle, St Basil says, "You sometimes ask and do not receive, because you ask rashly, or faithlessly, or lightly, or have asked things not profitable to you, or have not persevered."--S. Bas. Cons. Mon. cap. 1. vers. fin. You have asked "faithlessly," that is, with little faith, or with little confidence; "lightly," or with feeble desire of obtaining your request; "things not profitable to you," or not conducive to your salvation. St Thomas reduces to four, the conditions necessary to render prayer efficacious; namely, that a person pray for himself; that he ask for things necessary for salvation; that he pray with piety and with perseverance.--S. Thom. 2. 2. q. 83. a. 7. ad. 2.

The first condition then of prayer is, that it be offered for one's self. The angelic Doctor holds, that no one can efficaciously obtain eternal life for others, nor, by consequence, the graces appertaining to their salvation. Because, he says, the promise of Jesus Christ was made in favor of those who pray, and not of others: "He will give to you." However, many divines, resting on the authority of St Basil, maintain an opposite opinion. The holy Doctor teaches that by virtue of the divine promise, prayer infallibly produces its effect even in favor of others, provided they raise no positive obstacle to its efficacy. This doctrine is strongly supported by Holy Scripture. "And pray one for another, that you may be saved. For the continual prayer of the just man availed much."--St James 5:16. "Pray for them that persecute and calumniate you."--Matt. 5:44. "He that knows his brother to sin a sin which is not to death, let him ask, and life shall be given to him who sins not to death. There is a sin unto death; for that I say not that any man ask."--1 John 5:16. St Ambrose, St Augustine, venerable Bede and others say that by him who sins not to death, the apostle means a sinner who does not intend to live obstinately in sin unto death. The conversion of such a sinner requires a very extraordinary grace. But the apostle promises to him who prays for those that are not guilty of such enormous malice that they shall be converted. "Let him ask, and life shall be given to him who sins not to death."

However, it is quite certain, that the prayers of others are very profitable to sinners, and very pleasing to God. God complains of His servants, because they neglect to recommend sinners to His mercy, He once said to Mary Magdalen de Pazzi, "See my child, how sinners are in the hands of the devil: if my elect by their prayers did not deliver them, they should be devoured." The Almighty desires, in a particular manner that priests and religious pour forth their prayers in favor of sinners. Mary Magdalen de Pazzi used to say to her sisters in religion, "My dear sisters, God has separated us from the world not only to sanctify ourselves, but also to appease His wrath against sinners," The Lord one day said to her, "I have given to you my chosen spouses, a city of refuge, (that is, the passion of my Son) to which you may have recourse for the protection of my people. Recur then to that source of mercy, and procure assistance for my creatures who are perishing, and give your life for their salvation." Hence this saint inflamed with holy zeal, was accustomed to offer fifty times a day the blood of the Redeemer in behalf of sinners. So ardent was her desire of their conversion, that she frequently exclaimed, "How painful is it, O Lord, to see that I could assist your creatures by laying down my life for them, and that I am not allowed to do it." She recommended sinners to God in every duty, and it is recorded in her life that she scarcely allowed an hour to pass without presenting her fervent supplications for their return to God. She frequently rose by night, and prostrated herself before the blessed sacrament to pray for them. But, notwithstanding all these efforts of zeal, being once found bathed in tears, and being asked the cause of her weeping, she replied, "because it appears to me, that I do nothing for sinners." Such was her charity, that at her own request she was frequently visited by the Almighty with the sharpest pains and infirmities for the conversion of sinners: she even offered herself to be condemned to the pains of hell for their salvation, provided she could be confined to that place of torments without hating God. She prayed especially for priests; because their virtues ensure the salvation of many, and their bad examples causes the ruin of thousands. Hence, she frequently begged of God to punish her for their sins, saying, "Lord, put me to death frequently, and make me return to life, that by frequently suffering the pangs of death, I may satisfy your justice for them." It is related in her life, that she liberated numberless souls from the hands of Lucifer.

The zeal of this saint deserved particular notice. But no one can be animated with the love of God without praying continually for poor sinners. How is it possible that they who love God, and see His love towards man; who know what Jesus Christ has done and suffered for the salvation of the world, and how ardently He desires that we should pray for sinners; how I say, is it possible that they can look with indifference at the deplorable condition of so many poor souls separated from God, and groaning under the slavery of hell; or not be moved frequently to beseech the Almighty to give to those unhappy creatures light and strength to rise from the miserable state of perdition in which they slumber. It is true, that God has not promised to hear our prayers in their favor when they put a positive impediment to their own conversion. But God, in His goodness has been frequently induced by the prayers of His servants to bring back to the path of salvation, by extraordinary graces, the most blind and obdurate sinners. Let us, then be careful never to omit the recommendation of poor sinners to God in saying and hearing Mass, in our communions, meditations, and visits to the blessed Sacrament. A learned author says that he who intercedes for others will be the more readily heard when he prays for himself. Let us now return to the other conditions which St Thomas requires for the efficacy of prayer.

The second condition laid down by the holy Doctor, is, that we ask for "graces necessary for salvation." The promise of Jesus Christ to give whatever we pray for in His name does not extend to temporal favors, which are not necessary to salvation. St Augustine, explaining the words of Christ, "Whatsoever you ask in my name," etc. says that "whatever is opposed to our everlasting welfare is not asked in the name of the Redeemer." Sometimes we pray for temporal favors, and because God loves us, and desires to show us mercy, He does not attend to our petitions. "A Christian faithfully supplicating God for the necessaries of this life is sometimes mercifully heard, and sometimes, through mercy, his cry is disregarded; for the physician knows better than the patient what will mitigate his pains."-

-S. Aug. tom. 3, cap. 212. A physician does not administer to his sick friend a palatable remedy, which he knows would increase his malady. Oh! How many had they been visited with infirmity and poverty, would have abstained from sins which they committed in affluence and health. It is for this reason that God, seeing that health of body, and the goods of fortune, would be to some, an occasion of the loss of grace, or at least, of tepidity in His service, refuses to hear their prayers for these benefits. However, I do not mean to say that it is a fault to ask of God temporal blessings, as far as they are conducive to eternal salvation. "Give me," said the wise man, "only the necessaries of life."--Proverbs 30:8. According to St Thomas, it is not forbidden to entertain a well ordered solicitude for worldly goods. But it is criminal to desire and seek earthly riches with an inordinate affection--not as means of salvation, but as if we placed our supreme felicity in their possession. Whenever, then, we pray for such favors, we should ask them with resignation to the divine will, and on the condition that they be profitable to our souls; and when the Lord does not grant them, let us rest assured that He refuses them because He loves us, and because he knows they would be an obstacle to our spiritual welfare.

It often happens, that we beg of God to free us from some dangerous temptations; but He appears deaf to our cry, and permit's the enemy to continue to molest us. Let us be persuaded that this too is for our greater good. It is not by temptations and bad thoughts, but by a criminal consent to them that we are separated from God. By recommending herself to God in temptations, and by rejecting, with His assistance, the evil suggestions of her enemies, the soul makes rapid progress in perfection, and soon becomes intimately united with God; and therefore the Lord does not attend to her prayers, but suffers her temptations to continue. St Paul prayed with great fervor to be delivered from temptations of the flesh, but his prayer was not heard. "There was," said he, "given me a sting of the flesh, and angel of Satan to buffet me; for which thing thrice I besought the Lord, that it might depart from me; and He said to me: My grace is sufficient for you."--2 Cor. 12:7. Thus even in our temptations, we should pray with resignation; saying, if it be expedient, remove from me, O Lord, this temptation; if not, give me at least grace to resist it. And then, as St Bernard says if God does not grant us the favor we ask, He will bestow a more useful gift. To try our fidelity, and for our greater profit, God often permits us to be buffeted by the tempest. He appears deaf to our prayers; but no, He hears our cry, and secretly assists and fortifies us by His grace to repel every attack of the enemy. Behold how He speaks by the mouth of the Psalmist: "You call upon me in affliction: I heard you in the secret place of the tempest: I proved you at the waters of contradiction."--Psalm 80:8.

The remaining conditions of prayer are, piety and perseverance. Piety includes humility and confidence. Perseverance consists in continuing to pray unto death. As humility, confidence, and perseverance are the most necessary conditions of prayer, I shall speak of each separately.

CHAPTER IV

OF THE HUMILITY WITH WHICH WE OUGHT TO PRAY

The Lord regards the prayers of His servants who are humble: "He has had regard to the prayers of the humble."--Ps. 101:18. But to the prayers of the proud He does not attend; no, He rejects them with disdain: "God resists the proud, and gives grace to the humble." --St James 4:6. The Almighty does not hear the supplications of the proud who trust in their own strength, but leaves them to their own weakness and misery which when they are abandoned by divine grace, will infallibly lead them to perdition. "Before I was humbled," said holy David, "I offended."--Ps. 118:67., As if he said, I have sinned because I have not been humble. A similar misfortune befell St Peter. When this apostle was admonished by Jesus Christ, that on the night of His passion all the disciples should abandon Him their Lord and Master, instead of acknowledging his own weakness, and asking strength from above to remain faithful, he trusted in his own power, and exclaimed, "Although all shall be scandalized in You, I will never be scandalized."--St Matt. 26:33. Jesus said to him: Amen I say to you that in this night before the cock crow, you will deny Me thrice; Peter confiding in his own courage, rejoined boastingly, "Yes, though I should die with You, I will not deny You."--ver.35. And what was the result? Scarce had Peter entered the house of the high priest, when he three times denied the charge of being a disciple of Jesus, and to his denial added the solemnity of an oath. And again he denied with an oath, that "I know not the man."--Matt. 26:72. Had Peter been humble, and had asked of God the gift of constancy, he would not have denied his master.

Each one should consider that he is, as it were, on the top of a lofty mountain, suspended over the abyss of all sins, and supported only by the thread of God's grace; if this thread give way he shall infallibly fall into the abyss, and shall perpetrate the most enormous crimes. "Unless the Lord had been my helper, my soul had almost dwelt in hell."--Psalm 43:17. If God had not succored me, I would have fallen into numberless sins, and should now be buried in hell. Such were the sentiments of the Psalmist, and such should be the sentiments of each one of us. It was from a conviction of his own nothingness and misery, that St Francis used to say that he was the greatest sinner in the world. His companion, on one occasion, said to him, "Father, what you say cannot be true, surely, there are many greater sinners than you." "What I have said," replied the saint, "is too true, for if God had not preserved me, I would have committed sins of every kind."

It is of faith, that without the assistance of grace we cannot perform any good work, or even have a good thought. "Without grace," says St Augustine, "men do nothing whatever either by thought or action."--S Augus. de Corr. et Grat. cap 2. "As the eye cannot see without light," said the saint, "so we can do nothing without grace." "Not," says the apostle, "that we are sufficient to think anything of ourselves, as of ourselves; but our sufficiency is from God."--1 Cor 3:5. And the royal prophet says, "Unless the Lord build the house, they labor in vain that build it."--Ps. 126:1 In vain does a man labor to sanctify himself unless God assist him. "Unless," he says in the same Psalm, "the Lord keep the city, he watches in vain that keeps it."--Ibid. If God does not guard the soul from sin, in vain will man by his own strength endeavour to preserve her from its stain. Hence the Psalmist says, "For I will not trust in my bow."--Ps. 43:7. I will not confide in my own arms, but in

God, who is able to save me.

Hence, whosoever had done good, or has abstained from great sins, should say with St Paul, "By the grace of God I am what I am."--1 Cor 15:10., and ought to tremble, lest on the first occasion he should fall. "Wherefore he that thinks himself to stand, let him take heed lest he fall."--1 Cor 10:12. By these words the apostle insinuates that he who considers himself secure, is in very great danger of falling. For in another place he says, "if any man think himself to be something, whereas he is nothing, he deceives himself."--Gal. 6:3. Hence St Augustine wisely observes, "The presumption of stability renders many unstable; no one will be so strong as he who feels his own weakness."--Ser. 13 de verb. Dom. Whosoever says that he entertains no fear of being lost, betrays a pernicious self-confidence and security, by which he deceives himself. For, confiding in his own strength, he ceases to tremble, and being free from fear, he neglects to recommend himself to God, and left to his own weakness, he infallibly falls. For the same reason, everyone should be careful to abstain from indulging vain glory at not having committed the sins into which others have fallen; and should even esteem himself worse than them, saying, Lord if you had not assisted me, I would have been guilty of much more grievous transgressions. But if any one glory in his own works, and prefer himself before others, the Almighty, in chastisement of his pride, will permit him to fall into the most grievous and horrible crimes. The apostle says, "With fear and trembling work out your salvation."--Phil. 2:12. The timid distrust their own powers, and placing all their confidence in God fly to His protection in all dangers. He will enable them to overcome the temptations to which they are exposed, and they shall be saved. St Philip Neri walking one day through Rome, was heard frequently to say, "I despair."

Being corrected by a religious, he replied; "Father, I despair of being saved by myself, but trust in God." We should continually distrust ourselves, and thus we shall imitate St Philip, who was accustomed to say every morning as soon as he awoke. "Lord preserve me this day, otherwise I will betray You."

We may then conclude with St Augustine, that the great science of a Christian is to know that he is nothing, and that he can do nothing. "This is the great science, to know that man is nothing." A Christian who is convinced of his own nothingness will constantly seek and obtain from God by humble prayer the strength which he does not possess, without which he cannot resist temptation or do good, and with which he can do all things. "The prayer of him that humbles himself shall pierce the clouds: and he will not depart till the most high behold."--Eccles. 35:21. The prayer of a humble soul penetrates the heavens, and ascending to the throne of God, will not depart till it is regarded with complacency by the Almighty: and however enormous the sins of such a soul may be, the supplications of a humble heart cannot be rejected: A contrite and humbled heart, O God, You will not despise."--Ps 50:19. "God resists the proud and gives His grace to the humble."--St James 4:6. God treats the proud with scorn and refuses their demands; but to the humble He is sweet and liberal. This is precisely the sentiment which Jesus Christ one day expressed to St Catherine of Sienna: "Be assured, my child, that a soul who perseveres in humble prayer obtains every virtue."--Ap. Blos. In. Con. Cap. 3.

I shall here insert the beautiful observations addressed to those who aspire to perfection by the learned and pious Palafox, Bishop of Osma, in a note on the 18th letter of St Teresa. In that letter the saint gives to her confessor, a detailed account of all the degrees of supernatural prayer with which she had been favored. The bishop, in his remarks on the letter, observes that these supernatural graces which God deigned to bestow on St Teresa and other saints, are not necessary for the attainment of sanctity; since without them, many are arrived at a high degree of perfection, and obtained eternal life while many enjoyed them, and were afterwards damned. He says that the practice of the gospel virtues, and particularly of the love of God, being the true and only way to sanctity, it is superfluous and even presumptuous to desire and seek such extraordinary gifts. These virtues are acquired by prayer, and by corresponding with the lights and helps of God who ardently desires our sanctification."--Thess. 4:3.

Speaking of the degrees of supernatural prayer described by St Teresa, the holy bishop wisely observes, that as to the prayer of quiet, we should only desire and beg of God, to free us from all attachment and affection to worldly goods, which, instead of giving peace to the soul, fills it with inquietude and affliction. Solomon justly called them, "vanity of vanities, and vexation of spirit."--Eccl. 1:14. The heart of man can never enjoy true peace till it is divested of all that is not God, and entirely devoted to His holy love to the exclusion of every object from the soul. But man of himself cannot arrive at this perfect consecration of his being to God; he can only obtain it by constant prayer. As to the sleep of suspension of the powers, we should entreat the Almighty to keep them in a profound sleep with regard to all temporal affairs, and awake only to meditate on His Divine goodness, and to seek divine love and eternal goods. For all sanctity and the perfection of charity consists in the union of our will with the holy will of God. As to the union of the powers, we should only pray that God may teach us by His grace, not to think or seek, or wish anything but what He wills.

As to ecstasy or rapture let us ask the Lord to eradicate from our hearts inordinate love of ourselves and of creatures and to draw us entirely to Himself to the flight of the Spirit, we will merely implore the grace of perfect detachment from the world that like the bird which never rests on the earth, and feeds in its flight, we may never fix the heart on any sensual enjoyment, but by attending towards heaven, employ things of this world only for the support thereof. As to the impulse of Spirit, let us ask God courage and strength to do the violence to ourselves which may be necessary to resist the attacks of the enemy, to overcome our passions, or to embrace suffering even in the midst of spiritual dryness and desolation. Finally, as to the wound. As the remembrance of a wound is constantly kept alive by the pain it inflicts, we should supplicate the Lord to fill our hearts with His holy love to such a degree, that we may be always reminded of His goodness and affection towards us and thus we may devote our lives to love, and please Him by our works and affections. These graces will not be obtained without prayer; but by humble, confident, and persevering prayer, all God's gifts may be procured.

CHAPTER V

ON THE CONFIDENCE WITH WHICH WE OUGHT TO PRAY

The condition which St James insists on, as most indispensable for the efficacy of prayer is that we pray with a secure and unhesitating confidence of being heard. "But let him ask in faith, nothing wavering."--St James 1:6. St Thomas teaches, (S. Thom. 2. 3. q. 83. a. 2.) that "prayer derives from charity its virtue to merit a reward, and from faith and confidence, its efficacy to obtain the objects of our petitions." The same doctrine is inculcated by St Bernard, who says, that "confidence alone obtains mercy from the Lord." S Ber. Ser. 3. de. Annunc. Confidence in God's mercy is exceedingly pleasing to His divine Majesty, because it is a tribute of homage and praise to His infinite goodness, --the attribute which He wished particularly to manifest to the world by the creation of man. "Let all them," said the Royal Prophet, "be glad that hope in You: they shall rejoice forever, and You shall dwell in them."--Ps. 5:12. God protects and saves all who confide in Him: "He is the protector of all that trust in Him."--Psal. 17:31. "You who save them that trust in You."--Ps. 16:7. Oh! What splendid promises are made in the Holy Scriptures to all who hope in the Lord! Whosoever trusts in Him will not transgress the divine law. "And none of them that trust in Him shall offend."--Ps. 33:23. The Almighty keeps His eyes constantly fixed on those who confide in His goodness, to preserve them from the death of sin. "Behold," says David, "the eyes of the Lord are on them that fear Him, and on them that hope in His mercy to deliver their souls from death."-Ps. 32:18, 10. And again He says, "Because he hoped in Me, I will deliver him:

I will protect him: I will deliver him, and I will glorify him."--Ps. 90:14, 15. Mark the reason why God promises these favors: because, says the Lord, he confided in me, I will protect him; I will deliver him from his enemies, and from the danger of offending, and I will give him eternal glory. Isaias, speaking of those who put their trust in God, says, "But they that hope in the Lord, shall renew their strength, they shall take wings as the eagles, they shall run and not be weary, they shall walk and not faint."--Isaias, 40:31 They shall lay aside their weakness, and put on the strength of God; they shall not faint, nor even be fatigued in treading the rugged ways of salvation, but shall run and fly like the eagle. "In silence and in hope shall your strength be."--Isaias, 30:15. The holy prophet tells us that all our strength consists in placing our entire hope in God, and in silence, or in reposing peacefully in the arms of His mercy, casting away all confidence in our own efforts, or in human means.

And has it ever happened that he who trusted in God was lost? "No one has hoped in the Lord, and has been confounded."--Eccles. 2:11. David's confidence gave him a security of eternal life: "In You, O Lord, have I hoped, let me never be confounded."--Ps. 30:1. Is it possible that God should become a deceiver, and that after having promised support in their dangers to all who trust in Him, He should forsake them when they invoke His assistance. "God," says St Augustine, "is not a deceiver, who offers His protection and afterwards withdraws Himself from us, when we place our trust in Him." "Blessed is the man," says David, "that trusts in You." And why? Because, says the Psalmist, "mercy shall encompass him that hopes in the Lord."--Ps. 31:10. He is surrounded and protected on every side by the Almighty, and is secured against his enemies, and the danger of eternal damnation.

Hence the apostle exhorts us so earnestly, not to suffer our confidence in God to be impaired: "Do not therefore lose your confidence, which has a great reward."--Heb 10:35. The graces which we shall receive from God, will be proportioned to our confidence: if it be strong and free from wavering, they shall be abundant: "Great faith deserves a great reward." St Bernard compares the divine mercy to an immense fountain which gives out its salutary waters in proportion to the magnitude of the vessel of confidence in which they are to be carried: "You, O Lord," he says, "do not pour the oil of mercy, unless into vessels of confidence,"--S. Bern. Serm. 3. d. Annun. "Let Your mercy, O Lord," says the prophet, "be upon us as we have hoped in You."--Ps. 32:22. This was verified in the centurion, whose confidence was praised by the Redeemer: "Go," said our Lord to him, "and as you have believed, so be it done to you."--St Matt. 8:13. Our Lord once revealed to St Gertrude that they who pray with confidence, do violence to Him in such a manner, that they must be heard, and obtain whatever they ask. "Prayer," says St John Climacus, "piously does violence to God." Yes, prayer does violence to the Almighty; but it is a violence which is pleasing and acceptable to Him.

"Let us go, therefore," says St Paul, "with confidence to the throne of grace that we may obtain mercy, and find grace in seasonable aid."--Heb. 4:16. The throne of grace is Jesus Christ who sits at the right hand of His Father, not on a throne of justice, but of grace to obtain pardon for sinners, and perseverance for the just. To this throne we must always approach with confidence, but with that confidence which springs from a lively faith in the goodness, and in the veracity of God who has promised to hear those who pray with a secure and stable confidence. He that prays with diffidence, need not expect to be heard; "for," says

St James, "he that wavers is like a wave of the sea, which is moved and carried about by the wind. Therefore, let not that man think that he shall receive anything from the Lord."--St James 1:6,7. His prayer will not be regarded: the unjust diffidence by which he is agitated, renders the divine mercy deaf to his petitions. "You have not asked rightly," says St Basil, "because you have asked with diffidence." David said, that our confidence in God should be like a mountain, which receives unmoved the blast of the tempest. "They that trust in the Lord shall be as Mount Sion: he shall not be moved for ever that dwells in Jerusalem."--Ps. 124:1. The Redeemer strenuously exhorts us to pray with a firm confidence of obtaining what we ask: "Whatsoever you ask when you pray, believe that you shall receive; and they shall come unto you."--St Mark 11:24. Whatever favor you ask, have confidence that you shall receive it, and your prayer will be heard.

But you will say, on what can I a miserable sinner ground a secure confidence of obtaining whatever I ask? I answer, on the promise of Jesus Christ. "Ask," He says, "and you shall receive."--St John 16:24. "Who," says St Augustine, "can fear deception, when truth promises." Can we entertain any doubt of being heard, when the God of truth promises to grant whatever we ask. "He would not," says St Augustine, "exhort us to ask, if He did not intend to give." Now He constantly entreats and commands us in Holy Scriptures, to pray, to ask, to seek, to knock, and adds that "whatever we will, it shall be done unto us."--St John 15:7. To induce us to pray with suitable confidence, the Redeemer in the Pater Noster, the prayer which He Himself composed, has taught us to call God our Father, rather than Lord or Master, when we petition for the graces necessary for salvation; thus exhorting us to ask God's grace, with the same confidence, as a destitute sickly child, asks for food and medicine from a tender parent. If a father be informed of the miserable condition of a beloved Son who is dying from hunger, will he not instantly provide food for his starving offspring: if he be told that the child was bitten by a serpent, will he not make every effort in his power to apply the proper remedy.

Trusting then in the divine promises, let us pray with a confidence not wavering, but strong and firm. "Let us hold fast the confession of our hope, without wavering (for He is faithful that has promised)."--Heb. 10:23. Since it is of faith that God fulfills His promises, we should pray with a secure confidence of being heard, and should never be deterred from persevering in prayer by the absence of sensible confidence arising from spiritual dryness, or from the agitation produced by the commission of some fault. On the contrary, in the time of dryness and agitation we should even force ourselves to pray: for then, our prayers being accompanied with diffidence in ourselves, and proceeding from a confidence in the goodness and fidelity of God, who has promised to hear all who invoke Him, they will be very acceptable to Him and will be very readily heard. O how pleasing it is to the Lord to see us in the time of tribulations, of fear and temptations, hope against hope, or against that feeling of distrust which naturally springs from a state of desolation. For this reason the apostle praised the confidence of the patriarch Abraham, "who against hope believed in hope."--Rom. 4:18.

St John says that he who places a firm confidence in God, will certainly become a saint: "And everyone that has this hope in him sanctifies himself, as he also is holy."--1 John 3:3. For God pours His graces abundantly on those who trust in Him. This confidence enabled so many martyrs, so many tender virgins, and so many helpless children to withstand the savage cruelty of tyrants, and overcome the torments which had been prepared for them. We sometimes pray, but God appears not to heed us. Let us, on such occasions never abandon prayer, but let us rather redouble our confidence, saying with holy Job, "Although He should kill me I will trust in Him."--Job 13:15. O my God, though you should turn your face from me I will not cease to pray, and to hope in your mercy. Let us act in this manner, and we shall obtain from God whatsoever we desire. It was by perseverance in prayer after her petition had been repeatedly rejected that the Chananean woman obtained from Jesus Christ the object of her desires. Her daughter being possessed by a devil, she besought the Redeemer to deliver her, saying, "Have mercy on me, O Lord, You son of David: my daughter is grievously troubled by a devil."--St Matt. 15:22. Our Lord answered that He was not sent to the Gentiles, but to the lost sheep of the house of Israel. The woman was not dispirited by this reply, but came and adored Him, saying with confidence, "Lord, help me." He again answered, that "it is not good to take the bread of the children, and to cast it to the dogs." But she said, "Yes, Lord: for the whelps eat of the crumbs that fall from the tables of their masters." The Saviour seeing her great confidence, said to her, "O woman, great is your faith: be it done to you as you will."--Ibid. 25-27. "And no one," says Ecclesiasticus, "has ever invoked the Lord without obtaining relief. Or who has called upon Him, and He despised him?--Ecc. 2:12.

St Augustine called prayer the key which opens heaven to us; so that the favors we ask descend upon us the very instant our prayers ascend to God. "The prayer of the just man," he says, "is the key of heaven; his petition ascends, and God's mercy descends."--St Aug. Serm. 216. de temp. According to the royal prophet, our supplications and the divine mercy are inseparably connected. "Blessed," he says, "be God, who has not turned away my prayer nor His mercy from me."--Psalm 65:20. It is for this reason, that St Augustine tells us, whenever we pray, to have a secure confidence of being heard. "When," he says, "you see that you persevere in prayer, rest assured that the mercy of God is not far from you."--St Aug. in Ps. 95. For my part, I never feel more consoled in spirit, or more confident of salvation, than when I am employed in prayer, and in recommending myself to the divine mercy. I am sure the same may be said of all Christians. For it is a truth as certain and infallible as that God cannot violate His promises, that he who prays with confidence will be heard; but all other marks of our salvation are uncertain and fallible.

When we perceive our own weakness, and our inability to overcome some passion, or to surmount some difficulty, we should be careful not to imitate those pusillanimous souls who say, I cannot resist this temptation, I cannot discharge this duty, I cannot trust myself; but we should be animated by the example of the apostle, and say with him: "I can do all things in Him who strengthens me."--Philip. 4:13. Of ourselves we certainly can do nothing, but, with the divine assistance we can do all things. If the Almighty said to any of us, "Take this mountain on your shoulders and carry it; I will assist you;" would it not be folly and impiety to answer, I cannot move such an enormous weight; I will not attempt a task which I have not strength to perform. When then, we see that we are poor and miserable and wretched, and that we are encompassed with temptation, let us not be disheartened, but let us raise our eyes to heaven, and say with holy David, "The Lord is my helper: and I will look over my enemies."--Ps. 117:7. With the assistance of my Saviour I will overcome and despise all attacks of my adversaries. When we are in danger of offending God, or about to engage in any affair of importance, and know not what course to adopt or how to act, let us recommend ourselves to the Lord, saying, "The Lord is my light and salvation; whom shall I fear."--Ps. 26:1. And the Almighty will infallibly dissipate our darkness, and preserve us from every evil.

You will perhaps say, I am a sinner, and I have read in the scriptures that "God does not hear sinners."--St John 9:31. St Thomas answers with St Augustine, that these words were spoken by the blind man before he had been enlightened. "That," says St Thomas, "is the word of the blind man not as yet perfectly illumined, and therefore is not ratified."--St Thom. 2. 2. q. 83. art. 16. ad. 1. The angelic doctor adds that God indeed does not hear the supplications of sinners when their prayers proceed from a desire of persevering in sin; as for example, when they seek from God assistance to take revenge of their enemies, or to execute any other criminal design. The same may be said of sinners who while they pray for the means of salvation, have no desire to quit their sinful habits. There are some unhappy souls who even love the chains by which the devil keeps them in slavery. Their prayers are rash and abominable in the sight of God, and are therefore rejected. And what greater temerity can be conceived than to ask favors from a prince whom you have not only frequently offended, but whom you are determined still to offend. It is for this reason that the Holy Ghost says by the mouth of the wise man that the prayer of him who rejects the proffered knowledge of the divine commands is odious and detestable before the Lord: "He that turns away his ears from learning the law, his prayer shall be an abomination."--Prov. 28:9. To such sinners the Almighty declares that their prayers are unprofitable, that He will turn away from them, and will not attend to their supplications: "And when you stretch forth your hands, I will turn away my eyes from you, and when you multiply prayer, I will not hear."--Isaiah 1:15. It was thus He treated the prayer of Antiochus, who besought the Lord, and promised great things. But his promises were insincere, his heart was hardened in sin, his prayers proceeded from a fear of the chastisement with which he was threatened, and were therefore rejected by the Almighty. And he died a miserable death, eaten by worms that swarmed out of his body. "Then this wicked man prayed to the Lord of whom he was not to obtain mercy."--2 Macc. 9:13.

There is another class of sinners, who fall through human frailty, or through the violence of some passion; who ardently desire to shake off the yoke of the enemy, and fervently beseech the Almighty to burst the chains of death by which they are bound, and to deliver them from the miserable slavery of hell under which they groan. If they persevere in prayer, their cry will be infallibly heard by Him who has promised, that "every one that asks receives: and he that seeks finds."--Luc. 11:10. The author of the Imperfect Work, in his commentary on this passage, says that all sinners as well as saints receive what they ask, and find what they seek. (Auct. Oper. Imper. Thom. 18) The Redeemer says that what cannot be obtained from a friend for friendship's sake may be extorted by importunity: "Yet if he shall continue provoking, I say to you, although he will not rise and give him because he is his friend, yet because of his importunity he will rise, and give him as many as he needs. And I say to you, "Ask and it shall be given to you," etc--Luke 11:5-9. Thus persevering prayer obtains mercy from God, even for those who are not his friends. St Chrysostom says that "friendship is not so powerful before God as prayer: and what friendship has not accomplished, prayer effects."--St Chrys. Hom 56. St Basil teaches that "sinners obtain what they ask, if they ask with perseverance." St Basil Cons. Mon. cap. 1. St Gregory says, "Let the sinner cry aloud, and his prayer will reach the most high."--St Greg. in Ps. 6. Poenit. St Jerome observes that after the example of the prodigal child, who exclaimed, "Father I have sinned," every sinner may address the Almighty as his Father, provided he pray to be received again amongst the children of God.--S. Hierom. Ep. ad Dam. de Fil. Prod. St Augustine says, that "if God does not hear sinners, in vain would the publican have said, God be merciful to me a sinner,"--St Augus. trac. 24. In John. Now the gospel informs us that the publican by his prayer obtained pardon: "This man went down into his house justified."--St Luke 18:14.

The angelic doctor who has examined this point more minutely than any other writer does not hesitate to assert that God hears the prayers even of sinners; that though their prayers are not meritorious, still, since impetration depends on the goodness of God, and not on His justice, they have sufficient efficacy to obtain favors. "Merit," says St Thomas, "depends on justice, but impetration depends on grace."--St Th. 2. 2. 9. 83. a. 16. ad. 2. Hence Daniel implored the divine mercy, saying, "Incline, O my God, Your ear and hear: open Your eyes and see our desolation for it is not for our justification that we present our prayers before Your face, but for the multitude of Your tender mercies."--Dan. 9:18. To obtain then by prayer the graces we ask, it is not necessary to be the friends of God; by prayer we are restored to His friendship. "Prayer," says St Thomas, "makes us friends of God." St Bernard observes that the prayers of a sinner to be cleansed from his sin, proceed from a wish to return to God, now a desire to be converted to God is certainly the gift of heaven. And "why," says the saint, "would God inspire the sinner with such a desire if He did not intend to hear him." Hence so many examples recorded in the Holy Scriptures of sinners delivered from their sins by humble prayer. Thus Achab, (3 Kings,) Manasses, (2 Paral. 30.) Nabucodonozer (Dan.) and the good thief, (Luke 23:43) were restored by prayer to God's favor. O how wonderful is the efficacy of prayer. Two sinners die with Jesus Christ on Calvary; one begs of the Redeemer to remember him and he is saved, the other does not pray and he is damned.

In fine, St Chrysostom says, "No sinner has ever asked with sorrow the benefits of God without obtaining what he wanted." St Chry. Hom. de Moysi. But why seek further reasons or authorities when Jesus Christ has said, "Come to me all you that labor and are burdened, and I will refresh you."--Matt. 11:28. St Jerome, St Augustine, and others say that by them who "are burdened," the Redeemer meant sinners who groan under the weight of their iniquities and that if these invoke the Lord, they will according to the promise of Christ be refreshed, restored to His friendship, and saved through the divine mercy. "Ah," says St Chrysostom, "you do not desire so ardently the forgiveness of your sins as God desires to grant it." The saint adds that "there is no favor, which the most abandoned sinner may not obtain by fervent and assiduous prayer."--St Chrys. hom. 23. in Matt. Mark the words of St James: "But if any of you want wisdom, let him ask of God who gives to all men abundantly and upbraids not."--St James 1:5. The Lord then hears all who pray to Him, and enriches them with his graces: "Who gives to all men abundantly." The words, "and upbraided not," signify that God does not act like men, who when asked for a favor by one who had offended them, immediately upbraid him with his misconduct. It is not thus the Almighty treats those who ask His mercy. Though their sins be as numerous as the sands of the sea, or as the stars of the heavens, He will not reproach them with their iniquities when they ask any favor conducive to their eternal salvation, but as if they had never insulted His Majesty, He will instantly receive and console them. He will hear their supplications, and will enrich them abundantly with all His gifts. To animate our confidence the Redeemer says, "Amen, Amen, I say to you, if you ask the Father anything in my name, He will give it to you."--John 16:23; as if He said, sinners be not disheartened, let not your sins deter you from invoking my Father, and hoping to obtain from Him eternal salvation. You indeed have no claim to the graces which you require; you deserve nothing, but everlasting torments. But notwithstanding your unworthiness, go to my Father in my name, and through my merits ask the graces you stand in need of, and I promise, I even swear, to you, ("Amen, Amen, I say to you," is according to St Augustine, a species of oath,) that my Father will grant whatever you demand. O God! Can a sinner have a greater source of consolation than to know with certainty that he will receive all he asks in the name of Jesus Christ?

I say that he will obtain every thing which appertains to eternal salvation for with regard to temporal goods, I have already said that the Almighty does not always hear us when we pray for them, because He knows they would be opposed to our spiritual interests. But His promise to hear our prayers for spiritual favors, is absolute and unconditional; and therefore St Augustine exhorts us to ask with confidence of receiving them, the graces which God has promised absolutely. "What God has promised, ask with security."--Glossa. ex. Aug. ad. 2. Cor 13. And, how can God refuse what we ask with confidence when He is more desirous of dispensing His graces than we are of obtaining them? "He," says St Augustine, "is more willing to bestow His benefits on you, than you are to receive them."

St Chrysostom says that God's wrath is provoked against us only when we neglect to ask His gifts. "He is not angry except when we do not ask." Is it possible that God will not hear a soul imploring favors agreeable to His will? When a Christian says, Lord, I do not ask from you goods of this earth; I do not seek riches, honors, or pleasures; I only beg your holy grace; deliver me from sin, grant me a good death, inflame my heart with your holy love, (which, St Francis of Sales says should be more fervently asked from God than any of His other gifts;) infuse into my soul a spirit of resignation to your holy will; can the Almighty refuse to hear such a prayer? "What prayers, O Lord," says St Augustine, "will you hear, if you reject those that are according to your own heart?" Our confidence when we pray for spiritual favors should be animated by the words of Jesus Christ. "If you, then being evil, know how to give good gifts to your children, how much more will your Father from heaven give the good spirit to them that ask Him."--Luke 11:13. If you, says the Redeemer, who are so full of self-love, and therefore so much attached to your own interest, cannot refuse your children what they ask, how can your heavenly Father, whose love for you exceeds that of the tenderest parent; how I say, can He deny you the spiritual blessings which you seek from Him by humble prayer?

CHAPTER VI

ON THE PERSEVERANCE NECESSARY FOR PRAYER

Humility then, and confidence, are indispensably necessary for the efficacy of prayer, but to obtain final perseverance, and with it eternal life, they are not sufficient. Particular prayers will certainly obtain the particular graces which are sought from God, but to obtain final perseverance, we must continue in prayer to the end of our lives, because final perseverance includes the accumulation of many graces, and therefore requires multiplied prayers, and prayers continued unto death. The grace of salvation is not one grace alone, but a chain of graces, all of which are united with the grace of final perseverance. Now to this chain of graces, another chain of prayers ought to correspond; if by neglect of prayers we break the chain of our prayers, the chain of graces on which our salvation depends, will be also broken, and we shall be lost.

The Council of Trent, indeed teaches that we cannot merit the grace of final perseverance, and declares that "it can be had only from Him who is able to confirm those who stand so that they may stand perseveringly."--Sess. 6. cap 13. However, St Augustine says, that this great gift of perseverance can in some measure be merited; that is, it can be obtained by prayer. "This gift of God (perseverance) can therefore be suppliantly merited; that is, it can be obtained by supplication.--St Aug. de Don Perse. 6. And Suarez adds, that whoever prays will infallibly receive it. But St Thomas teaches that to obtain perseverance and to be saved, unceasing and continual prayer is necessary. "To enter heaven," he says, "continual prayer is necessary after baptism.--St Thom. 3. p. q. 39. a. 5. The same doctrine is taught in many passages of the New and Old Testament. "We ought always to pray and not to faint."--Luke 18:1. "Watch you, therefore, praying at all times, that you may be accounted worthy to escape all these things that are to come, and to stand before the Son of Man."--Luke 21:36. "Let nothing hinder you from praying always."--Eccl. 28:22. "Bless God at all times: and desire Him to direct your ways."--Job 4:10. It is for this reason the apostle exhorted his disciples to continual prayer. "Pray without ceasing."--Thess. 5:17. "Be constant in prayer, watching in it with thanksgiving."--Coloss. 4:2. "I will therefore that man pray in every place."--1 Tim 2:8. The Lord ardently desires to bestow on us the gift of perseverance and eternal life, but says St Nilus, He will grant them to him only who prays with perseverance. "He wishes to confer His benefits on him who perseveres in prayer."--St Nilo. de. Orat. cap. 32. Many sinners are converted by divine grace, and obtain the pardon of their sins; but because they neglect to pray for perseverance, they relapse into their former, or greater sins, and lose all the fruit of their repentance.

Cardinal Bellarmine says that it is not sufficient to ask a few times, the grace of perseverance; but that to obtain it, we must pray for it daily and continually till death. "To obtain it every day, it must be sought daily." Whoever asks it today, will obtain it for today; but he that does not pray for it tomorrow, will fall on tomorrow. To inculcate the necessity of perseverance in prayer was the object of the Redeemer in the parable of the friend, who refused to give the loaves that were asked of him, till after the most importunate demands. "Yet if he shall continue knocking, I say to you, although he will not rise and give, because he is his friend; yet because of his importunity, he will rise and give him as many as he needs."--Luke 11:8. "Now," says St Augustine, "if to be freed from importunity, such a friend gave even against his will, the loaves that were asked of him, how much more will the God of goodness, who exhorts us to ask, and who is offended when we do not ask, give what we seek from Him." How much more readily will fervent and persevering prayer obtain the graces of the God of mercy, who being infinite Goodness eagerly desires to diffuse His benefits, and even entreats and commands us under pain of incurring His displeasure to pray them? The Almighty, then is most willing to grant us salvation, and the graces necessary for it; but He requires that we demand them with perseverance and even with importunity. Cornelius a Lapide in his comment on the above cited passage, says that "God wishes us to persevere in prayer, even to importunity." To men the importunate are intolerable, but God not only bears our importunity, but entreats us to seek incessantly and importunately His graces, and especially the gift of holy perseverance. St Gregory says that "God wishes to be invoked, He wishes to be compelled, He wishes to be overcome by a certain importunity. Happy violence, by which God is not offended, but is appeased."--St Greg. Hom. 1. in. Evan.

Thus to obtain perseverance, it is necessary to recommend ourselves continually to God, morning and evening, in our meditations, at mass, communion, and at all times, but particularly in the time of temptation, saying: Assist me, O Lord; assist me. O Lord, keep your hand upon me; do not abandon me; have pity on me. Is there anything more easy than to say, assist me, O Lord; assist me? On the words, "With me is prayer to the God of my life," the glossa says, "A person may say, I am unable to fast or to give alms; but if he be told to pray, he cannot say I am unable to pray;" because there is nothing more easy than to pray. But to procure the divine aid, we must never cease to pray, we must continually do violence to heaven, that violence which is dear and agreeable to God. "This violence," says Tertullian, "is delightful to God." St Jerome declares that our prayers are pleasing to God in proportion to our perseverance and importunity. "Prayer, as long as it is importunate is the more acceptable."--St Hiero. in Luke 2.

"Blessed is the man that hears Me, and that watches daily at my gates."--Prov 8:34. Happy, says the Lord, is the man who hears me, and watches incessantly by holy prayer at the gates of my mercy. Isaias says, "Blessed are all they that wait for Him."--Isaias 30:18. Blessed are they who pray unto death expecting salvation from the Lord. Mark the language in which the Redeemer exhorts us to pray; "Ask and it shall be given you, seek and you shall find, knock and it shall be opened to you."--Luke 11:9 To inculcate the necessity of prayer, it would be sufficient to have said, "ask." Why then did He add, "seek" and "knock?" The latter words were certainly not superfluous; by them the Saviour wished to teach us that we should imitate the poor, who live upon the alms of the rich, who when refused what they asked, repeat their demands, and when the doors of the rich are closed against them, continue to knock till they become troublesome by their importunity. Thus God desires that we should pray, and never cease to pray for His succor and assistance, His light and strength, to preserve us from ever losing His holy grace. The learned Lessius says that whoever is in the state of sin, or in danger of death, and neglects to pray, or whoever neglects prayer for a considerable time, such as for a month of two, cannot be excused from a grievous fault. Moreover, he who is attacked by any grievous temptation, sin grievously, without doubt, if he seek not from God assistance to repel it; for otherwise he exposes himself to the proximate and even certain danger of falling.

You will perhaps ask, why God who desires to give me the grace of perseverance, does not grant it the first time I ask it? The holy Fathers assign many reasons God does not bestow the gift of perseverance as soon as it is asked, first, because He wishes to prove our confidence. Secondly, because He wishes that we should esteem highly and desire it earnestly. "God," says St Augustine, "does not wish to grant at once, that you may learn ardently to desire great things: what is long desired, is highly valued when obtained; what is easily given, is despised."--St Aug. Ser. 61. Alis. 5. de verb. Dom. Thirdly, that we may not forget Him; if we were already assured of perseverance and salvation, and had not further need of God's assistance to preserve His grace, we should soon forget Him. Want compels the poor to frequent the houses of the rich. Hence the Lord to draw us to Himself, (as St Chrysostom says) and to see us frequently at His feet that He may confer greater benefits upon us, defers the grace of salvation to the time of our death. "Nor does He defer it because He rejects our prayers; but because He wishes to render us by this means more careful in His service, and thus draw us to Himself."--St Chry. hom. 30. in Gen. Fourthly, that persevering in prayer, we may be more closely united with Him by the sweet chains of love. "Prayer," says St Chrysostom, "which accustoms us to converse with God, is a strong bond of divine love."--St Chry. in Ps. 4. O how the constant application to God by prayer, and the confident expectation of receiving from Him the graces we stand in need of, enkindle in us the fire of divine love, and unite us to the divinity.

But how long must we continue to pray? St Chrysostom answers, that we must pray until we receive the sentence of eternal salvation, that is till death. "Do not," he says, "desist, till you receive."--St Chry. hom 24. in Matt. 7. And he adds, that whoever is resolved to persevere in prayer until he receives a favorable sentence, will certainly be saved. "If," he says, "you shall say, I will not retire until I shall have received, you shall certainly receive."--(Ibid). "Know you not," says the apostle, "that they who run in the race, all run indeed; but one receives the prize? So run that you may obtain."--1 Cor. 9:24. It is not sufficient then to pray for salvation, it is necessary to pray always, until we obtain the crown which God promised, but promised to those only who are constant in prayer unto the end.

If then we wish to be saved, we must imitate the conduct of holy David, who kept his eyes always turned to the Lord, imploring the divine assistance and protection to escape the snares of his enemies. "My eyes are ever towards the Lord, for He shall pluck my feet out of the snare."--Psalms 24:15. "Because your adversary the devil, as a roaring lion, goes about seeking whom he may devour," (1 Peter 5:8) you should have your arms continually in your hands, to defend yourselves against his attacks, saying with the prophet, "I will pursue after my enemies, and overtake them; and I will not turn again till they are consumed."--Psalms 17:38. I will continue the combat till I shall see my adversaries vanquished. But how shall we be able to obtain so important and difficult a victory? St Augustine answers, "by most persevering prayer; by incessantly pouring forth our supplications as long as the combat shall last." "Since," say St Bonaventure, "the battle never ceases, let us never cease to ask for mercy." As we must fight continually so to escape defeat we must constantly seek the divine aid. Woe to them who in the time of battle gives up prayer. "Woe," says the wise man, "to them that have lost patience."--Eccl. 2:16. The apostle tells us, that "we shall be saved, if we hold fast the confession and glory of hope unto the end;" (Heb. 3:6) if we continue to pray with confidence, unto death.

Encouraged then by the mercy and promises of God, let us say with the same apostle, "Who then shall separate us from the love of Christ: shall tribulation? Or distress? Or danger? Or persecution? Or the sword?"--Rom 8:35. Who shall separate us from the love of Christ? Shall tribulation? Or the danger of losing the goods of this earth? Or the persecutions of devils or of men? Or the torments or sword of tyrants? "In all these things we overcome, because of Him that loved us."--Ibid. 37. No, said the apostle, neither tribulation, nor distress, nor danger, nor persecution, nor torments, can separate us from the love of Jesus Christ. Fighting for the sake of Him who gave His life for us, we shall, with the divine assistance, overcome all our enemies. Father Hyppolitus Durazz(sp) fearing, on the day he resolved to give up the dignity of Roman prelate, and to consecrate himself entirely to God in the Society of Jesus that he would be unfaithful on account of his weakness, said to the Lord Almighty, "Do not desert me." "Lord, do not abandon me, now that I have given myself entirely to You." The Lord answered him, saying, "I pray you not to desert me." And the servant of God trusting in the divine goodness and power, exclaimed, "Then you, O my God, will not abandon me, and I will not abandon you."

To conclude, if we wish not to be forsaken by God, we must never cease to pray that He may not abandon us. If we continually beg His grace, He will most certainly assist us, and will never permit us to be lost, or to be separated from His love. And to secure this constant aid from heaven, let us take care not only to seek incessantly the gift of final perseverance, and the graces necessary to obtain it, but also to beg by anticipation of the Lord, that great gift which He promised to His elect by the mouth of the prophet,"--the grace to persevere in prayer: "And I will pour out upon the house of David, and upon the inhabitants of Jerusalem, the spirit of grace and of prayer."--Zac. 12:10. Oh! How great a gift is the spirit of prayer, or the grace to pray always. Let us then never cease to ask from God this grace and spirit of constant and assiduous prayer. If we be forever constant in prayer, we shall certainly obtain the gift of perseverance, and every favor we desire; for God cannot violate His promise, to hear all who invoke His assistance. "For," says St Paul, "we are saved by hope."--Rom. 8:24. If we have a firm hope of persevering to the end in continual prayer, we may consider our salvation secure. "Confidence," says venerable Bede, "will afford us a wide entrance into this city."--Beda. Ser. 18. de Sanctis. Hope will give us a secure entrance into the kingdom of paradise.

ABRIDGMENT OF THE SECOND PART

God wills that all men be saved, and that no one perish; he exhorts and commands all sinners to repent and to be converted to Him; His Son has died for all, even the lost sheep of the house of Israel. He therefore bestows on all abundant means of salvation; to the just he either gives sufficient strength to persevere in justice, or the grace of prayer by which that strength may be procured, to sinners, even the most obdurate, He grants sufficient grace to return to His service, or at least, the grace of prayer by which they can, if they will, obtain the helps necessary for their conversion.

Since it has been clearly proved, in the first chapter of the first part, that prayer is necessary for the attainment of salvation, we must suppose that each one has from God sufficient aid (without requiring any other special grace) to enable him actually to pray, and by prayer to obtain all the graces necessary to observe unto death the divine commands, and thus merit eternal life. Thus, whoever is lost cannot ascribe his damnation to the want of helps necessary for salvation. As, in the natural order, God has ordained that man should be born naked, and destitute of the means of subsistence, and has given to him powers of mind and of body by which he can procure raiment and all the other necessaries of life, so in the supernatural order, men are born powerless, and incapable of obtaining by their own strength, eternal life; but God, of His own goodness, grants to them the grace of prayer by which they can obtain all the graces necessary for the observance of the divine precepts, and for eternal salvation. When I assert that God gives to all assistance, by which (without the aid of any other new grace) they can actually pray, I do not mean to say that assisting grace is not requisite for prayer; for I know that to perform any act of piety, besides the exciting grace of God, His assisting or cooperating grace is indispensably necessary. But, I say that without the aid of any new preventing grace which determines the will of man to actual prayer, the grace common to all enables each one to pray actually.

God wills that all men be saved, and that no one perish. "I desire therefore first of all, that supplications, prayers, etc., be made for all men. For this is good and acceptable in the sight of God our Saviour who will have all men to be saved, and to come to the knowledge of truth."--Tim 2:1-4. "We must," says St Prosper, "sincerely believe and profess that God will have all men to be saved; since the apostle who has said so, commands supplications to be made to God for all."--St. Pros. Resp. ad. 2. Objec. Vincent. "If," says St Chrysostom, "God desires the salvation of all men, it is our duty to pray for all. If He wishes all to be saved, let us endeavour to cooperate with His holy will."--St Chry. In 1 Tim 2 Hom. 7. "As I live, said the Lord God, I desire not the death of the wicked, but that the wicked turn from his way and live."--Ezec. 33:11. The Lord, then, says, and as Tertullian observes, because He desires to be believed, He even swears, that He wills not the death but the life of the sinner. "For," says David, "wrath is in His indignation; and life in His good will."--Psalms 29:6. If He chastises us, it is because our sins provoke His anger; but our salvation, and not our perdition, is the object of His most ardent desires. St Basil explaining the words, "and life in His good will," says that, "God wishes all to be made partakers of life." Again, the royal prophet says, "Our God is the God of salvation: and of the Lord, of the Lord are the issues from death."--Psalms 67:21. "It is," says Bellarmine in his comment on this passage, "peculiar to our God; it is His nature to be a God of salvation, and a God from whom proceed the issues of death, or deliverance from damnation." Thus the characteristic attribute of God is to save and to deliver all from eternal death.

    God invites and commands all sinners to return to Him. "Come to me," says the Redeemer, "all you that labor, and are burdened, and I will refresh you."--Matt. 11:28. "Not willing that any should perish, but that all should return to penance."--2 Peter 3:9. Since then, the Lord calls all to eternal life, and wills not that any should perish, He must have a sincere desire for the salvation of all. "Behold," He says, "I stand at the gate and knock. If any man hear my voice, and open to me the door, I will come in to him."-- Apoc. 3:20. "Why will you die, O house of Israel?..Return you and live."--Ezec. 18:31-2. "And then come and accuse Me, says the Lord: If your sins be as scarlet, they shall be made white as snow."--Isaiah 1:18. "What is there that I ought to do more to my vineyard that I have not done to it?"--Isaiah 5:4. "How often would I have gathered together your children as the hen does gather her chickens under her wings, and you would not.?"--Matt. 23:37. How could the Lord say that He stands knocking at the hearts of sinners? How could He exhort them to return to His embraces? How could He upbraid them saying, what more ought I to do for your redemption? How could He have said that He often wished to gather them together, as the hen gather her chickens, if He had not a sincere and ardent desire of their eternal happiness, and if He had not afforded them abundant means, at least by prayer of obtaining everlasting glory. St Luke says, that "Jesus Christ seeing the city, He wept over it."--Luke 19:41. "And," says St Chrysostom, "why did He weep when He saw the ruin of the Hebrews, but because He ardently desired their salvation!"

Jesus Christ has died for all men, and has offered to His eternal Father for each one, the price of His Redemption. "The Son of Man is come to save that which was lost."--Matt. 18:11. "Who gave Himself a redemption for all."--1 Tim 2:6. "And Christ dies for all that they also who live, may not now live to themselves, but unto Him who died for them."--2 Cor. 5: 15. "For therefore we labor and are reviled, because we hope in the living God, who is the Saviour of all men, especially of the faithful."--1 Tim. 4:10. "And He is the propitiation for our sins; and not for ours only, but also for those of the whole world."--1 John 2:2. "He that spared not even His own Son, but delivered Him up for us all, how has He not also with Him given us all things."--Rom. 8:32. If God has given His son for all, how can He deny them the helps necessary for salvation. If with His son He has given us all things, how can He refuse us the kingdom prepared for us from the beginning of the world?

Since, then, the Redeemer ardently desires that all men be saved, and that no one perish; since He calls on all sinners, and commands them to return to Him; and since He has offered His blood for their redemption; is it not evident that He bestows on all abundant means of salvation? In vain would the Lord stand at the door and knock, if, by His grace, He did not enable the sinner to open. In vain would He expect His vineyard to produce grapes, if He did not refresh it with the dews of heaven; and when the Lord should say, "what more ought I to do for the vineyard?" The sinner, if he had not at least the grace of prayer by which he could obtain the aid necessary for eternal life, might answer, that he had not produced fruit, because God had not given him the necessary means. In vain would the Almighty invite and exhort sinners to repentance if He did not bestow upon them the helps necessary for their conversion, or at least the grace of prayer, by which these helps might be procured. In vain would Jesus Christ have died for all sinners, if they had not assistance from above, by which they could repent of their sins, and receive the fruit of His blood.

"God," says the apostle, "is faithful, who will not suffer you to be tempted above that which you are able; but will make also with the temptation issue that you may be able to bear it."--1 Cor. 10:13. And the Council of Trent, adopting the language of St Augustine, has declared, that, "God does not command impossibilities, but by commanding, He admonishes you to do what you can, and to ask what you cannot do, and He assists you that you may be able to do it."--Sess. 6. c. 13. The holy Council, then to establish against the Reformers that the observance of the divine commands is not impossible to any one, has declared, that all men have grace to do good, or at least the grace of prayer by which they can procure greater help to do it. "By our faith," says St Augustine, "which teaches that the God of justice and of goodness cannot command impossibilities, we are admonished what to do in things that are easy, and what to ask in things that are difficult."--St Aug. de nat. & grat. cap. 69. Thus according to the council of Trent, it is in the power of each one to observe the divine commands, or at least to obtain by means of prayer, the graces necessary for their fulfillment. If then, God has given His law to all, and has made its observance possible to all at least by means of prayer, we must necessarily conclude that all receive the grace of prayer. And as the Lord by means of prayer gives actual grace to do good, and thus renders all His precepts possible, so He bestows on all the actual grace of prayer: otherwise, the man who should not receive the actual grace of prayer, could not obtain even by prayer, the aid necessary for the observance of the divine commands, and therefore, to him their observance would be utterly impossible.

St Basil says, that "when any one is permitted to fall into temptation, God enables him to bear with it, and to seek by prayer the will of God."--St Bas. Lib. Mor. Summar. Sum,. 62, cap. 3. "No one," says St Chrysostom, "can be excused for not having overcome the enemy, as long as he ceases to pray."--St Chrys. Hom. De. Moysi. Now, if he who is conquered by the enemy, had not the grace necessary for actual prayer, his defeat would be excusable, and could not be imputed to him. "Who are we?" Says St Bernard, "or what is our strength? God wished that we, seeing that we are deficient, and that we have no other means of assistance, should with all humility, have recourse to His mercy."--St Ber. Ser. 5. de Guadag. The Almighty, then has imposed a law upon us which of ourselves we are unable to observe that we may have recourse to him by prayer, and obtain strength to fulfill its precepts. But, if the grace of actual prayer were denied to any one, the observance of the law would be impossible to him. "Many, says St Bernard, "complain that grace is wanting to them; but God has much greater reason to complain that many are wanting to His grace."

St Augustine says, that "God imposes some precepts which we cannot fulfill to teach us what we ought to ask from Him." Again he says, "What then is shown to us, unless that to ask, and to seek, and to knock, is given by Him who commands us to do these things."--St Augus. lib. 1, ad Sempli. qu. 2. And again he says, "If you are not as yet drawn to God, pray that you may be drawn."--Idem Tract. 26, in john. num. 2. In another place, he says, "The soul knows not what to do, because she has not as yet received; but she will receive if she shall make a good use of what she has received: but she has received grace seek piously and diligently, if she will."--Ibid. cap. 22, n.

85. Then, everyone has the grace necessary for prayer, and whoever corresponds with it shall obtain grace to do that which was before above his strength. The same Father says in another place, "The man who wills, but cannot let him pray that his will be sufficiently strengthened to fulfill the precepts; for he is thus assisted to do what is commanded."--St Aug. de prat. & lib. arb. T. 10, n. 31, in fi.. And again he says, "God commands that we fatigued on account of our weakness by our efforts to fulfill the precepts, may learn to ask the assistance of grace."--1 Epis. 89. He says in another place, "It is certain that we shall observe the commandments if we will; but because the will prepared by the Lord, we must beseech Him to strengthen our will to such a degree that by willing we may fulfill the law."--De grat. et lib. arb. cap. 16. The holy Doctor then teaches that it is certain that if we wish, we shall observe the divine precepts, but that to desire to comply with our obligations, and to fulfill them in effect, prayer is necessary. The grace of prayer, therefore, and the grace to obtain by prayer abundant aid to discharge their duties is given to all. For if the grace to pray actually were wanting to any, they could neither fulfill the law, nor wish to fulfill it. To those who said they were unable to avoid evil or to do good, the holy Father answered, "But when they do nothing, let them pray for that which they have not as yet received."--Lib. de Cor. & Gra. cap. 2. n. 4. And, if they had not the grace of prayer, how could they by their petitions obtain that strength which they had not as yet received?

That God gives to all the grace by which they can actually pray, and by prayer obtain the helps necessary for salvation, appears from the precept of hope which obliges all to expect from God eternal life. For if God did not bestow on all the grace necessary for actual prayer, no one, without a special revelation, could comply with his obligation of hoping for eternal salvation from the divine mercy. The virtue of hope is so dear to God that He has declared that He takes complacency in those who trust in Him. "The Lord takes pleasure in them that hope in His mercy."--Psalm 146:11. He promises to all who hope in Him that they shall overcome their enemies that they shall persevere in His grace, and obtain eternal glory. "Because he hoped in Me I will deliver him: I will protect him: I will deliver him, and I will glorify him." --Psalm 90:14-15.;"He will save them because they have hoped in Him."--Psalm 36:40. "Preserve me, O Lord, for I have put my trust in You."--Psalm 15:1. "No one has hoped in the Lord and has been confounded."--Eccl. 2:11. And we know that heaven and earth shall pass away, but the promises of God can never fail. "Heaven and earth," says the Lord, "shall pass away, but My word shall not pass."--Matt. 24:35. "The whole merit of man," says St Bernard, "consists in placing all his hopes in God."--St Ber. Ser. 15. in Ps. 90. For they who hope in the Lord, honor and adore His divine majesty. "And call upon Me in the day of trouble: I will deliver you, and you shall glorify."--Psalm 49:15. He that confides in the Almighty, honors and adores the divine power, and mercy, and veracity; because by hoping for eternal life, from the divine goodness, he believes that God is able and willing to save him, and that he cannot be wanting to His promises to save all who trust in Him. The Prophet assures us that the mercy of God will be poured upon us in proportion to our confidence in His goodness. "Let Your mercy, O Lord, be upon us as we have hoped in You."--Psalm 32:22.

Now this divine virtue is so pleasing to the Lord, that He has imposed upon us a strict and grievous obligation of hoping in His mercy: "Trust in Him all you congregation of people."--Psalm 61:9. "You that fear the Lord hope in

Him."--Eccl. 2:9. "Hope in your God."--Osee, 12:6."Trust perfectly in the grace which is offered you."--1 Peter 1:13. "But our hope, to be pleasing to God, must be firm and certain: "Hope," says St Thomas, "is a certain expectation of beatitude."--St Th. 2. 2. q. 18. ar. 4.; and the Council of Trent says that, "all ought to place and repose a most firm hope in the divine assistance; for if they be not wanting to His grace, God as He began the work will finish it, enabling them to will and to perform." "For I know," says St Paul, "whom I have believed, and I am certain that He is able to keep that which I have committed unto Him."--2 Tim. 1:12. It is in its certainty that the hope of Christians differs from that of worldlings. The hope of worldlings is always uncertain, and cannot be otherwise, since it depends on the word of weak and fallible men who may be unable or unwilling to redeem their pledge, and may therefore, fail in the performance of their promise. But Christian hope is certain on the part of God, who is able and willing to save us, who has promised salvation to them who observe His law, and has also promised to all who ask them, the graces necessary for its observance.

It is true, as the angelic doctor says, that hope is accompanied with fear; (Ibidem, d. 3.) but this fear does not arise from any apprehension that the divine promises will not be fulfilled, but from a conviction of our own frailty, which exposes us to the danger of not corresponding with the divine grace, and of violating the divine law. The Council of Trent, therefore, has justly condemned the doctrine of the reformers who, because they denied free will to man, asserted that every Christian ought to have an infallible certainty of perseverance and salvation. This error was condemned by the Council of Trent, because as I have already stated to obtain salvation our correspondence with God's grace is necessary, and this correspondence is always uncertain and fallible. Hence, to secure us against the danger of presumptuous confidence in our own strength, the Lord wishes on the one hand that we should be always afraid of ourselves; and to preserve in our souls a firm and certain confidence in His goodness, He desires on the other that we entertain a full conviction of His good will, and of receiving His assistance whenever we seek it. St Thomas says that trusting in the divine power and mercy, we should expect with certainty eternal happiness from God: "Whosoever has faith is certain of the power and mercy of God."--Ibidem, a, 2.

Since then, our hope in God should be certain, we must have sure and infallible grounds of hope. For if the foundation of our hope were uncertain, we could not hope with certainty to receive from God eternal life, and the graces necessary for its attainment. But St Paul teaches that he who desires to be saved should be firm and immovable in hope: "If so you continue in the faith, grounded and settled, and immovable from the hope of the gospel which you have heard."--Col. 1:23. And in another place he says that our hope being founded on the promises of God, should be immovable as a secure and firm anchor: "And we desire that every one of you show forth the same carefulness to the accomplishing of hope unto the end; that by two immutable things in which it is impossible for God to lie, we may have the strongest comfort who have fled for refuge to hold fast the hope set before us which we have as an anchor of the soul, sure and firm."--Hebrews 6:11, 18. Hence St Bernard says that our hope cannot be uncertain, because it rests on the promises of God: "Nor does our expectation appear vain, or our hope doubtful, since we rely on the promises of eternal truth."--St Ber. Ser. 7. in Ps. 90. V. 1. And in another place, speaking of himself, he says that his hope depends on the charity with which God adopted us as His children, on the truth of His promises, and on His ability to fulfill them: "I consider three things in which my hope consists: the charity of adoption, the truth of promise, and the power of fulfillment."--St Ber. Ser. 3. Dom. 6. post Ben. n. 6.

It is for this reason that St James tells us that if we expect the graces of God, we must demand them, not with hesitation, but with a secure confidence that our petition shall be heard: "But let him ask in faith, nothing wavering. For he that wavers is like a wave of the sea which is moved and carried about by the wind. Therefore let not that man think that he shall receive anything of the Lord."--St Jas. 1:6, 7. And St Paul praises the faith of Abraham who, convinced of the infallibility of God's promises placed an unbounded and unhesitating confidence in them. "In the promise also of God he staggered not by distrust; but was strengthened in faith, giving glory to God; most fully knowing that whatsoever He has promised, He is able also to perform."--Rom 4:20,21. Jesus Christ tells us that we shall receive all the graces we desire when we ask them with a secure confidence of obtaining them: "Therefore I say unto you, all things whatsoever you ask when you pray, believe that you shall receive, and they shall come unto you."--Mark 11:24. In a word, God will not attend to our prayers, unless we believe with certainty that they shall be heard.

Our hope then of salvation should be certain as far as it depends on God. The grounds of this certainty are as we have already seen the power and mercy of God, and His fidelity to His promises. But the strongest and most certain of these three is the infallibility of God in the performance of the promises which He has made through the merits of Jesus Christ to save us, and bestow upon us the graces necessary for salvation. For although the power and mercy of God are infinite, still we could not expect with certainty eternal life from Him, if He had not infallibly promised it to us. Now, it is clear from the scriptures that God has promised eternal life only on the condition that we pray for it: "Ask and you shall receive.--If you ask the Father anything in My name, He will give it you.--We ought always to pray.--If anyone wants wisdom, let him ask of God." That the promise of God to bring us to everlasting glory is conditional may be proved by all the passages from the scriptures, and from the writings of the Fathers by which it was demonstrated in the first chapter of the first part that prayer is a necessary means of salvation.

Now if we were not certain that God gives to all grace by which (without requiring any other special grace not common to all), they can actually pray, what security or foundation could we have in God for hoping with certainty for eternal happiness? The grounds of hope arising from the power and mercy of God and His fidelity to His promises should in that case be doubtful and uncertain. When I am certain that by prayer I shall obtain eternal life, and all graces necessary for it, and that God (since He grants it to all) will not deny me the grace to pray actually, if I wish, then I have a secure and infallible ground of hoping salvation from Him, provided I be not unfaithful. But when I am uncertain whether God will give me the particular grace which He does not grant to all, and which is necessary for actual prayer then the foundation of my hope in God is doubtful, and that hope which according to the apostle should be immovable, firm, and secure, is utterly destroyed. The fulfillment then of the precept of hope, by which all are bound requires that all, even the most hardened sinners, should have at least the grace by which they can actually pray, and by prayer obtain all the helps necessary for salvation. I have been anxious to establish this point, first, in honor of the divine Providence; secondly, to assist and encourage those sinners who in consequence of the enormities of their sins might imagine that they were altogether forsaken by God, and altogether destitute of His grace, and might therefore abandon themselves to despair; and thirdly, to take away every excuse from those who say they are unable to resist the attacks of the flesh and of the devil, by demonstrating to them that all the damned are lost through their own fault, and that God gives to each one the grace of prayer by which, if he will, he can obtain strength to overcome concupiscence and every temptation. But my principal object has been to inculcate to all the use of this most powerful and necessary means of prayer that all who desire to be saved, may hereafter attend to it with greater diligence and zeal. For it is because they do not pray or apply for the divine assistance that so many poor souls lose the grace of God, continue to live in sin, and in the end are damned. And notwithstanding the necessity of this great means of salvation, the greater number of preachers and of confessors, seldom exhort their auditors or penitents to the practice of prayer, without which it is impossible to observe the law of God, or to obtain the gift of perseverance in His grace.

Being convinced of the absolute necessity of prayer, inculcated in numberless passages of the old and new testament, I have introduced into the missions of our congregation a rule, which has been observed for many years, and which prescribes that in every mission a sermon be preached on prayer. And I say, and I repeat, and I will repeat while I live that our salvation depends altogether on prayer; that on that account all writers in their books, all preachers in their sermons, and all confessors in the tribunal of penance, should inculcate nothing with greater zeal than the practice of continual prayer, and that they should constantly exclaim and repeat: Pray, pray and never cease to pray. For if you pray, your salvation is secured; if you neglect prayer, your perdition is inevitable. Such should be the practice of all preachers and confessors since all Catholics maintain that he who prays will infallibly obtain grace, and will be saved. But the number of those who practice prayer is very small, and therefore but few obtain eternal life.

APPENDIX

A PRAYER TO OBTAIN FINAL PERSEVERANCE

Eternal Father, I humbly adore you, and thank you for having created me, and for having redeemed me through Jesus Christ. I thank you most sincerely for having made me a Christian by giving me the true faith, and by adopting me as your son in the sacrament of baptism. I thank you for having after the numberless sins I had committed, waited for my repentance, and for having pardoned (as I humbly hope) all the offences which I have offered to you, and for which I am now sincerely sorry, because they have been displeasing to You, who are infinite goodness. I thank You for having preserved me from so many relapses of which I would have been guilty, if you had not protected me. But my enemies still continue, and will continue till death to combat against me, and to endeavor to make me their slave. If you do not constantly guard and succor me with your aid, I, a miserable creature shall return to sin, and shall certainly lose Your grace. I beseech you then for the love of Jesus Christ to grant me holy perseverance unto death. Jesus, your Son, has promised that You will grant whatsoever we ask in His name. Through the merits then of Jesus Christ, I beg for myself and for all the just, the grace never again to be separated from Your love, but to love you forever in time and eternity. Mary, Mother of God, pray to Jesus for me.

A PRAYER TO JESUS CHRIST TO OBTAIN HIS HOLY LOVE

O My dearest Jesus, my crucified love, I believe and confess that you are the Son of God and my Saviour. From the abyss of my nothingness, I adore You, and I thank You for the death You have suffered to obtain the life of divine grace. My beloved Redeemer, to You I owe my salvation. Through You, I have until now been preserved from hell; through You I have received the pardon of my sins. But I, an ungrateful wretch instead of loving You, have again offended You. I have deserved to be condemned to that place in which I could never love You. O my Jesus, chastise me in any way You please, but not with the privation of Your love. If in my past life I have not loved You, I am sincerely sorry, and now I love You, and desire nothing in heaven or on earth, but to love You with my whole heart. But, without Your aid I can do nothing. Since, then, You command me to love You, give me grace to fulfill so sweet and lovely a precept. You have promised to grant whatsoever we ask of You. "Whatsoever you will, ask, and it will done unto you." Trusting then in this promise, O my dearest Jesus, I ask in the first place the pardon of all my sins which I detest above all things, because they have offended You who are infinite Goodness. I ask holy perseverance in Your grace unto death. But above all, I ask the gift of Your holy love. Ah! My Jesus, my hope, my love, and my all, inflame me with that fire of love which You came on earth to enkindle. Light up in my soul the fire of Your love, and grant that I may always be resigned and conformable to Your holy will. Enlighten me to see continually still better how much You deserve to be loved, and to comprehend the immense love You have borne to me, but especially when You gave Your life for me. Give me then the grace to love You with my whole heart, to love You continually and to seek constantly in this life the grace to love You that persevering in Your holy love unto death, a day may come when I shall love You with all my strength in heaven, and shall never cease to love You for all eternity. O Mother of love, Mary, my advocate and refuge, you who are the most lovely of all creatures, and the most beloved of God; you are the most ardent lover of God, and desire nothing but to see Him loved by all. Ah, through the love which you bear towards Jesus Christ, pray for me, and obtain the grace to love Him forever, with my whole heart. From you I ask this favor, from you I hope to receive it. Amen

A PRAYER TO OBTAIN CONFIDENCE IN THE MERITS OF JESUS CHRIST, AND IN THE INTERCESSION OF MARY

Eternal Father, I thank You from the bottom of my heart, on my own behalf, and on behalf of the human race, for the great mercy You have shown to us, in sending Your Son to assume human flesh and to die, in order to obtain for us eternal life. I thank You for this great mercy, and in thanksgiving for it, I desire to love You as much as so great a favor deserves. Through His merits which have satisfied Your justice, for the punishment due to us, You pardon our faults; through them, you receive into favor, miserable sinners who deserve nothing but your hatred, and everlasting fire; through them, You admit worms of the earth into the kingdom of your glory; through them, in fine, You have bound Yourself to grant every favor which we ask in the name of Jesus Christ.

I thank You also, O infinite Goodness, who, to strengthen our confidence, have, beside Jesus Christ whom You have sent as our Redeemer, also given us for our advocate Your beloved daughter Mary, that she, with that heart which you have given to her, full of mercy, might continually succor, by her prayers, every sinner who has recourse to her; that she might assist them by that intercession which you have made so powerful before your divine Majesty, that you know not how to refuse any favor which she asks of You.

It is Your will that we will place great confidence in the merits of Jesus, and in the intercession of Mary. But this confidence is Your own gift; it is a great gift which You give to them only, whom You wish to save. This confidence, then, in the Blood of Jesus, and in the patronage of Mary, I ask of You through the merits of Jesus and of Mary. To You also do I cry, O dear Redeemer, who to obtain for me confidence in Your merits, have sacrificed Your life on the cross. Accomplish, then, the end for which you died: grant that, trusting in Your passion, I may hope all things. And you, O Mary, my Mother, and my hope after Jesus Christ, obtain for me a firm confidence in the merits of your Son, and, in your omnipotent prayers, by which you obtain from God whatsoever you ask. O my beloved Jesus. O my sweet Mother, Mary, to you who have so tenderly loved me, I confide and consign my soul: have pity on me, and save me.

Devout Acts to be made in the Visit to the Blessed Sacrament, and to the image of the Blessed Virgin Mary

In public Visits made by the people, these Acts will be read aloud by the Priest, and will be repeated by the people.

O My soul, excite your faith and confidence. You stand before the infinite majesty of your God, who, for the love of you, came down from heaven; who became man, and died on a cross for your salvation; who now remains in the

Holy Sacrament to hear you, and to grant all the graces you ask of Him. Speak to Him, then and say,

AN ACT OF FAITH AND OF ADORATION

O My God, because You have revealed that You are the infallible truth, I believe whatsoever the holy church proposes to my belief.   I believe that You are the sovereign Lord of heaven and earth, that You will reward the good with eternal happiness, and will punish the wicked with everlasting torments. I believe that in You who are one only God, there are three divine persons, the Father, the Son, and the Holy Ghost. I believe, O adorable Son of God, that You have become man in the womb of Mary; that You died on a cross for our salvation; and that at this moment, You are present in the Most Holy Sacrament, to nourish us with Your flesh in the Holy Communion, and to hear our prayers when we visit Your altars. Prostrate, then, at Your feet, I, a miserable sinner, though unworthy to appear before You, and deserving only of everlasting fire, adore Your infinite Majesty, uniting my adoration with that which the angels and saints, along with the most holy Mary, render to You.

AN ACT OF HOPE

O My dear Redeemer, trusting in Your almighty power, confiding in Your infinite goodness and mercy, and in the promises You have made us, I firmly hope, through the merits of Your passion, to obtain the pardon of my sins, perseverance in Your grace till death; and finally, I hope to see and to love You eternally in heaven.

AN ACT OF CHARITY

O My God, because You are infinitely good, and worthy of

infinite love, I love You with my whole heart and above all things, and I desire to see You loved by all men, as much as You deserve to be loved." I rejoice that You are, and will be infinitely happy for eternity.

AN ACT OF CONTRITION

O My beloved Redeemer, if for Your sake I had abandoned all things, and had spent my life in the desert; if I had died in the midst of torments for the love of You, surely all this would be nothing in comparison of the bitter death which You condescended to suffer for me. But how have I treated You for the past? I have repaid You with ingratitude: instead of loving You, I have frequently offended Your majesty, and turned my back upon You, by ungratefully despising Your grace and Your love. I repent, O my Jesus, and am sorry from the bottom of my heart, for having offended You who are infinite Goodness. O that I had been dead sooner than have insulted Your majesty. I hate and detest all the injuries I have offered to You. I promise and purpose, for the future, to die rather than ever offend You more: I likewise resolve to receive during my life, and at the hour of my death, the Holy Sacraments. The remainder of my life, whether it be short or long, I desire, O infinite Majesty, to spend in loving You my only good, who are amiable above every good. But of what use will these promises be, O God of my soul, if You do not succor me? Without Your assistance, I will betray You again, and will offend You still more grievously than I have hitherto done. I seek and hope through the merits of your passion, the grace of perseverance; grant it me, O Lord, and never permit me to be separated from You again: may I die sooner than ever lose Your grace and become Your enemy.

AN ACT OF THANKSGIVING

O my Jesus, I thank You for all the graces You have bestowed upon me; for having created me, for having redeemed me with Your blood, for having made me a Christian by Holy Baptism, for having borne with me so long while I continued to offend You. If I had died in my sins, I should now be in hell, I should be lost, O my God, and could never love You. I thank You, then, for having waited for me with so much patience, for having (as I hope) so mercifully pardoned me. I thank You particularly for having left me Your precious body in the most holy sacrament, for having so frequently given me Yourself for the food and nourishment of my soul, and for now admitting me into Your holy presence. I thank You for all Your favors, and I hope I shall thank You for them for all eternity in heaven, where I expect to sing Your mercies for ever.

AN ACT OF OBLATION

O My Jesus, You have suffered a painful and ignominious death for the love of me; You have shed the last drop of Your blood for my redemption. What return can I make for so much love? I can do nothing more than offer You my entire being. Yes, O Lord, I offer and consecrate myself entirely to You. I give You my soul, my body, and my will, resigning myself in all things, and forever, to Your most holy will. Do whatever You please with me. Only make me love You in this life, and in the next; and then dispose of me, and of all that I possess, in whatever way You choose. Tell me what You wish from me, and, with the assistance of Your holy grace, I will do it.

PRAYER

I recommend to You, O Lord, the Sovereign Pontiff, and all Bishops and Priests; give them that spirit which will enable them to sanctify the whole world. I recommend to You all infidels, heretics, and sinners: grant them light and strength to abandon sin, and to consecrate themselves entirely to the love of You, who are infinite goodness. I recommend to You all who are in their last agony, my parents, benefactors, and friends: and I recommend to You, in an especial manner, all my enemies, because you command me to do it. Make them happy, O Lord, in this life, and glorify them in the next. I recommend to You the souls in Purgatory: alleviate their pains, and shorten the time of their banishment, that they may soon enjoy Your glory in heaven.

Finally I beg, O Jesus, that from that throne of love on which You are seated in this tabernacle, You will, through Your merits, grant to me a deep and sincere sorrow for my sins, and full pardon of all the offences I have ever offered to You. Grant me holy humility and meekness, that I may bear with patience all contempt and persecutions. Grant me grace to practise that mortification which You desire. Give me perfect resignation to Your will, so that I may cheerfully embrace all crosses which come to me from Your holy hands. Give me light to know, and strength to execute Your holy will. Give me a great confidence in Your most holy passion, and in the patronage of Mary Your blessed mother. Give me the great gift of Your holy love, and a strong desire to love You, so that I may always say, O my God, I desire to enjoy You alone, and nothing else. Give me strength to persevere in Your love till death, and never to lose Your holy grace. Above all, I beseech You to give me the grace to seek continually this holy perseverance, by always recommending myself to You and to Your blessed Mother, especially by constantly saying, when I am tempted, Jesus and Mary, Jesus and Mary, assist me. Eternal Father, for the love of Jesus Christ, grant me all these graces.

SPIRITUAL COMMUNION

O my Jesus, I love You with my whole heart, and I desire to be forever united to You. Since I cannot receive you sacramentally, I desire to receive You spiritually. Come then to my soul; I desire to embrace You, I unite myself entirely to You, and I beseech You never to permit me to be separated from You.

[Here the Litany of the blessed Virgin, and the following Hymn, with the V. R. and Prayer, &c. are to be said.]

THE HYMN, PANGE LINGUA.
In English.

Sing, O my tongue, adore and praise
The depth of God's mysterious ways:
How Christ, the world's great king, bestow'd
His flesh, conceal'd in human food,
And left mankind the blood that paid
The ransom of the souls he made.

Giv'n from above, and born for man,
From Virgin's womb his life began;
He liv'd on earth, and preach'd to sow
The seeds of heav'nly truth below;
Then seal'd his mission from above
With strange effects of power and love.

'Twas on that evening when this last
And most mysterious supper past,
That Christ with His disciples sat,
To close the law with legal meat;
Then to the twelve himself bestow'd
With His own hands, to be their food.

The Word made flesh, for love of man,
By His word turns bread to flesh again;
And wine to blood unseen by sense,
By virtue of omnipotence:
And here the faithful rest secure,
Whilst God can vouch, and faith insure.

TANTUM ERGO

To this mysterious table now our knees, our hearts, and sense we bow: Let ancient rites resign their place To nobler elements of grace; And faith for all defects supply, While sense is lost in mystery.

To God the Father, born of none, To Christ, his co-eternal Son, And Holy Ghost, whose equal rays From both proceed, one equal praise: One honor, jubilee, and fame, Forever bless His glorious name.' Amen

V. You have given them bread from heaven. Alleluia.
R. Replenished with all sweetness and delight. Alleluia.

Let us Pray
O God, who has left us in this wonderful sacrament, a perpetual memorial of Your passion; grant us, we beseech You, so to reverence the sacred mysteries of Your body and blood, that we may continually find in our souls the fruit of

Your redemption: who livest and reigns, &c.

VISIT TO MARY, MOTHER OF GOD

O Great Queen of Heaven, most holy and immaculate Virgin Mary, I, a miserable sinner, salute you from this earth, and venerate you as the Mother of God. Among all creatures you are the most beautiful, the most holy, the most amiable, and the most beloved by God. I love you, O my Mistress, above all things after God, and I desire to see you loved by all. I rejoice at your glories, and I thank the Lord for your great exaltation. I thank you, O my Mother, for all the favors you have obtained for me from God, during the whole course of my life. I dedicate myself to your service forever, and I put myself under your protection. Accept me, O my Queen, and do not reject me as my sins deserve. I know that you are so powerful before God, that he never refuses any favor you ask from him. O Mother of mercy and refuge of sinners, into your hands I consign my soul; Ah! Have pity on me. Recommend me to your Son, and obtain for me the pardon of all my sins, the gift of divine love, and strength to persevere, to live, and to die in God's grace. Above all, I beg of you to obtain for me the grace to recommend myself always to you, and particularly when I am tempted to offend God. Assist me always in life, and in death. O my Mother, I confide in you. My salvation depends on the merits of Jesus your Son, and on your intercession. I hope through them to be saved; may I not be confounded. Amen.

THE HYMN, PANGE LINGUA.
In Latin.

Pange lingua gloriosi Corporis mysterium,
Sanguinisque pretiosi, Quem in mundi pretium
Fructus ventris generosi, Rex effudit Gentium.

Nobis datus, nobis natus Ex intacta Virgine,
Et in mundo conversatus, Sparso verbi semine;
Sui moras incolatus, Miro clausit ordine:
In supremae nocte coenae, Recumbens cum fratribus,
Observata lege plene Cibis in legalibus;
Cibum turbae duodenae Se dat suis manibus.
Verbum caro, panem verum Verbo carnem efficit;
Fitque sanguis Christi merum Etsi sensus deficit;
Ad firmandum cor sincerum
Sola fides sufficit.

Tantum ergo sacramentum
Veneremur cernui:
Et antiquum documentum
Novo cedat ritui;
Praestat fides supplementuin
Sensuum defectui.
Genitori, Genitoque
Laus & jubilatio,
Salus, honor, virtus quoque
Sit & benedictio;
Procedenti ab utroque
Compar sit laudatio. Amen.

Vers. Panem de coelo praestitisti eis. Alleluia.
Resp. Omne delectamentum in se habentem, Alleluia.
Oremus.

Deus, qui nobis sub Sacramento mirabili passionis tuae memoriam reliquisti, tribue quaesumus, ita nos corporis & sanguinis tu sacra mysteria venerari; ut redemptionis tuae fructum in nobis jugiter sentiamus, Qui vivis & regnas, &c.

THE HYMN, ADORO TE DEVOTE

I Devoutly adore You, O hidden Deity, Which lies concealed indeed under these forms;
To You my whole heart subjects itself,
Because it finds itself quite lost in contemplating You.
The sight, the feeling, and the taste, are here deceived,
But the hearing alone maybe safely believ'd; I believe whatever the Son of God has spoken;
Nothing can be more true than the word of truth.
Upon the cross the divinity alone was concealed;
But here the humanity also lies hid.
Yet I believe and confess both the one and
the other, And make the same petition as did the penitent thief.
I don't here see Your wounds, as Thomas did,
Yet I confess You to be my God. O grant that I may ever believe in You more and more.
And evermore put my trust in You, and love You.
O blessed memorial of the death of our Lord,
O living Bread, giving life to man,
Grant that my soul may ever live on You;
Grant that I may ever relish thy sweetness.
O pious pelican, Jesus our Lord,
Cleanse me, an unclean sinner, with Your blood;
One drop of which is sufficient to save
The whole world from all its guilt.
O Jesus, whom I now see under a veil,
O when will that 'hour come,
which I so much long for!
When the veil being removed, I shall see
Your face, And be happy for ever in the contemplation of Your glory. Amen.

THE END.

Other Titles in Print that can be purchased through
St Athanasius Press

The History of Heresies and Their Refutation
by St Alphonsus Liguori

The Practice of Religious and Christian Perfection
3 Volume Set by Fr Alphonsus Rodriguez, S.J.

The Raccolta or a Manual of Indulgences

Vera Sapentia or True Wisdom by Thomas A Kempis

1910 Benziger Catalog Church Ornaments of our own Manufacture

A Thought From Thomas A Kempis for Each Day of the Year

Dignity and Duties of the Priest or Selva by St Alphonsus Liguori

www.stathanasiuspress.com

www.ingramcontent.com/pod-product-compliance
Ingram Content Group UK Ltd.
Pitfield, Milton Keynes, MK11 3LW, UK
UKHW041412180426
11947UKWH00007B/87